5/14/24

1—

DELI

DELI

101 New York-style deli dishes from chopped liver to cheesecake

by Sue Kreitzman

A Particular Palate Cookbook ™
Harmony Books/New York

For Abe Lebewohl of the Second Avenue Delicatessen and Leo Steiner of the Carnegie Delicatessen— Upholders of the tradition

A Particular Palate Cookbook

Published by Harmony Books, a division of Crown Publishers, Inc., One Park Avenue, New York, New York 10016 and simultaneously in Canada by General Publishing Company Limited

HARMONY, PARTICULAR PALATE, and colophons are trademarks of Crown Publishers, Inc.

Manufactured in the United States of America

Library of Congress Cataloging in Publication Data

Kreitzman, Sue.
    Deli: New York-style deli dishes, from chopped liver to cheesecake.

    "A Particular palate cookbook."
    Includes index.
    1. Cookery, American—New York (State)   2. Delicatessen.
3. Cookery, Jewish,   I. Title.
TX715.K8974 1985   641.59747   84-945
ISBN 0-517-55701-0

10 9 8 7 6 5 4 3 2 1

First Edition

Contents

Acknowledgments

Many people acted as guides, teachers, and advisors during the development of this book. My gratitude toward Abe Lebewohl of New York's 2nd Avenue Deli and Leo Steiner of New York's Carnegie Deli is unbounded. Abe fed me many delicacies and led me through the lower depths of his deli where tongues and briskets cure in huge vats of solution. Leo fed me more delicacies and expounded, fascinatingly, on the history and prehistory of Jewish food. Both patient men answered an unending succession of questions, supplied recipes, and explained techniques and ingredients.

In addition, an equal amount of unbounded affectionate gratitude goes to:

Mark Russ Federman of Russ and Daughters on the Lower East Side. Mark, as the son of a Russ daughter and the third generation proprietor of the famous family store, knows all there is to know on the rich subject of the "appetizing store." His advice has been invaluable.

Jerry Goldsmith of the Cornucopia Deli on New York's Upper West Side. Jerry opened his deli because he decided that the neighborhood was suffering from "ethnic food nostalgia." His mother's chicken soup, served every day at the deli, would warm a marble heart, and I am delighted to have the recipe for this collection.

Lavish thanks too, to the following:

Harry Zaidel, ("Harry-the-Pickle"), of the Premier Pickle Company in Norcross, Georgia; Fay Robinson and Georgia Richardson of the Quality Kosher Deli in Atlanta; Tony Patak of Patak's Meats in Austell, Georgia; Gerald Cooper, that paragon of patience and wisdom at Morton's Salt; Merle Ellis; Dr. Stanley Green at F.D.A.; Arthur Kirsch of Kirsch's Mushrooms in the Bronx; Stanley Zimmerman of Sammy's Roumanian Steak House in New York; Lee Levrey; Wolfgang Puck of Spago in Los Angeles; Simon and Sammy Engelman of Engelman's Bakery in Atlanta; and Monte Weiner of the Carnegie Deli.

A special thank you to those loyal friends who were always willing to dine at my house during testing time, even though dinner might be seven soups or four corned beefs. Charlie and Ruth Ann Little, and Margaret and Terry Pedersen were always game to try one of these bewildering meals.

And finally, a large and heartfelt thank you to my family: my husband, Steve, who plumbed his deepest culinary memories for suggestions for this collection and who supplied the voice input interface to our trusty word processor; and to my son, Shawm, who shaped the bagels, solved the mystery of the kaiser rolls, and filled the house with music. And my beagle, Shallot, despite his advanced years, continued to assure me that I am the best cook in the world. Thanks, Shallot.

Introduction

Everyone has a personal version of soul food—a culinary system of emotional time travel that returns the diner to an earlier, less complicated age. Proust bit into a madeleine. I prefer a hot dog. My earliest food memory is of eating a sizzling, fleshy, bursting-with-juice frankfurter, under a crunchy tangle of sauerkraut in a mustard-slathered bun. As my baby teeth sank through the skin of that mythic sausage, it went k-nock! (you pronounce the *k*) and the juices ran down my chin. The bun disintegrated, the mustard oozed over everything, and my budding gastronomic exhilaration increased, until the meal ended in an orgy of impassioned finger licking. More than forty years later, its tastes and textures are still vivid and unforgettable.

I grew up on New York deli food. That quintessential frankfurter was only the beginning. I remember scorchingly hot, golden-crisp crinkle-cut fried potatoes; towering sandwiches of crackly crusted, caraway-studded sour rye piled with succulent, brilliantly seasoned pastrami or corned beef; and boiling-hot soup so thick with beans and barley and wild mushrooms that a spoon would stand straight up in the bowl. There were omelets that enfolded morsels of spicy salami or silken smoked salmon; pungent bits of pickled herring in creamy, onion-strewn sauce; and hot bagels, thickly spread with chive-flecked cream cheese and topped with ruby-red slices of beefsteak tomato. Cabbage leaves in sweet-and-sour raisin sauce held hidden riches of finely ground beef and veal, made tender with matzoh meal and fragrant with cinnamon and nutmeg. Hamburgers rested in poppy-seed-dusted buns under a mantle of caramelized shreds of sweet onion. Cheesecake caressed the tongue with creamy-smooth, lemon-haunted sweetness.

This is my culinary heritage, the soul food that—in adulthood—chases the collywobbles on blue days, restores coping abilities in times of stress, and never fails to satisfy both emotional and physical hungers.

For this book, I have gathered together lots of classic deli recipes. Some have been reconstructed from my memories of childhood deli meals; others come from generous deli proprietors in New York, where I began eating, and Atlanta, where I continue to eat. There are even a few recipes that I like to think of as "nouvelle deli"—Wolfgang Puck's smoked salmon pizza, for example. Or my own smoked fish mousse and souffléed challah French toast. These dishes and a few more like them maintain the integrity of the deli taste, but bring in a dimension of elegance and lightness.

If your early food memories, like mine, are of meltingly tender kugels, nut-crusted coffee cakes, gloriously sour pickles, and all the rest of it, you will fall into the aura of this collection of recipes as into a safe haven. If, on the other hand, the whole deli experience is alien to your background, you are about to begin an exciting gastronomic adventure. *Ess gezunt!*

WHAT IS DELI? Jewish deli food has become a firmly established and well-loved component of America's melting-pot culture. Many people think that deli food *is* Jewish food, but it is only one small part of a complicated cuisine. Jewish food encompasses an enormous range of geographic influences and ethnic legacies. Styles of cookery from all the regions of the world that have housed Jews, modified and unified by the powerful thread of Jewish dietary law, make up the vast culinary hodgepodge that is Jewish cookery. Because of these widely different styles of cuisine, one Jew's soul food may well be another's *chozzerai,* or junk food.

Delicatessens began to appear in New York around the turn of the century. The first delis were not restaurants at all. They were shops selling Eastern European and German Jewish meat delicacies. "Specials" (large frankfurters), pastrami, cured tongue, and corned beef were offered, along with breads and salads. Eventually, chairs and tables were added, baked beans (Heinz vegetarian) and French fries rounded out the menu, and delis became full-fledged restaurants.

Jewish dietary law forbids mixing meat and dairy products, so delis never sold or served cheeses, butter, milk, or the like. Instead, separate Jewish dairy restaurants opened, serving Eastern European and German dairy dishes. While delis dispensed thick meat sandwiches and fat hot dogs, dairies sold such things as cheesecakes, cream soups, and sour cream dishes. Under dietary law, certain foods are considered *pareve,* compatible with both dairy and meat. Eggs and fish fall into this category and were offered in both types of restaurants. In the meantime, "appetizer" stores sprang up. Appetizer stores (often called appetizing stores today—ungrammatical but apt) sell smoked, cured, and pickled fish and all manner of salads and appetizers.

As the century progressed, the dietary boundaries that kept each kind of food emporium unique began to blur. Non-Jews became passionately fond of both deli and dairy food. Many Jews relaxed their orthodoxy. Soon nonkosher Jewish-style delis came into existence, serving dishes from both the deli and the dairy, with plenty of appetizing specialties thrown in for good measure. Substantial dinner classics of German Jewish and Eastern European Jewish origin—stuffed cabbage, potato pancakes, kugels, and so on—found their way onto the menu as well.

Now, deli food is going the way of all American ethnic foods. There are Jewish-style delis all over the country, but a frightening percentage of them feature matzoh balls from jars, canned potato pancakes, jarred and canned soups, frozen kasha varnishkes, presliced frozen lox—it's enough to break a traditionalist's heart. It gives me great pleasure, therefore, to present this book, which I consider a chronicle of vanishing deli tradition.

Equipment, Ingredients, and Basic Recipes

EQUIPMENT There are a few pieces of endearing and enduring old-fashioned kitchen utensils that are essential to deli cookery. Try to find *a wooden chopping bowl* and *a hand chopper*. This kitchen duo is exactly right for chopped liver, chopped herring, gefilte fish, hard-boiled-egg mixtures, and halvah mousse, and the *chop chop chop* is good exercise. (A food processor or blender results in a texture that is too fine.) I own an old bowl and chopper that belonged to my grandmother. Similar ones can still be found in many cookware shops.

A four-sided grater is a must for grating onions and potatoes. For other vegetables, the grating disk on a food processor works just beautifully. And the processor's slicing disk is perfect for preparing cabbage for soup, coleslaw, or sauerkraut.

A fine-mesh sieve is needed for puréeing split pea soup, straining chicken soup, draining yogurt for cheese, and smoothing out cottage cheese. If you have trouble finding a sieve or strainer with a fine-enough mesh, try a *tamis* from a restaurant supply shop.

You must have *a steamer* for heating slices of cooked corned beef and pastrami. No other method produces the proper degree of authentic deli succulence. The least expensive and easiest to store is the kind of steamer that resembles a standing metal basket made out of perforated petals. The basket can be used in a wok or a saucepan. Even better is a large stockpot fitted with a removable perforated steamer insert. This, of course, will be much more expensive than the small adjustable basket, but it will also be much more versatile. You will use the stockpot again and again, with and without the steamer insert.

A FEW WORDS ON INGREDIENTS

Dried mushrooms. The pungent and spongy dried *Boletus edulis* is vital to several of the recipes in this book. The mushrooms, known as *porcini* in Italy, *cepes* in France, *steinplitze* in Germany, and *borowicki* in Poland, are available by the ounce in many gourmet and specialty shops around the country, but it is much more economical to buy them in bulk through the mail (see the Source Guide, page 94). In a pinch you can pick up 1-ounce clear plastic containers of dried mushrooms in some delis and in the ethnic-food departments of some supermarkets. The mushrooms will very likely be *Boletus luteus* from South America—not as fine as *Boletus edulis,* but they'll do.

An ounce of dried mushrooms goes a long way. When reconstituted, they plump up to at least five times their dried weight. The flavor, then, will be up to twenty times as intense as that of an ounce of the same mushroom in the *undried* (or *fresh*) state. Kept scrupulously dry in a tightly covered glass jar, they will keep forever. During very hot and humid weather, refrigerate the jar.

Dried mushrooms harbor quantities of sand and grit in their nooks and crannies. Always rinse them well in cold water before reconstituting. After soaking, rinse them again and strain off the soaking water through a sieve lined with a coffee filter or several layers of cheesecloth. *Never* discard the soaking water. It is a rich essence of mushroom that should be incorporated into the dish being prepared, or saved to enrich future soups, stews, or gravies.

Flour. Three kinds are required for various recipes in this book: unbleached, bread flour, and self-rising. Always measure flour, no matter what kind, in the following manner: set a 1-cup dry measure on a sheet of wax paper. Spoon flour lightly into the measure until the cup is overflowing. Level off the flour with a knife and dump into a bowl. Repeat (using smaller measures when needed at the end) until the required amount of flour is in the bowl. Pick up the wax paper, fold, and tip the leftover flour back into the flour bag.

Horseradish. Horseradish is a powerful root. Scraped and grated, it is used as an accompaniment to gefilte fish and an ingredient in several dairy dishes. Hand grating the root produces the same physical symptoms as an emotional crisis: a red, snuffly nose, streaming bloodshot eyes, and throbbing sinuses. A food processor or blender makes things a little easier. Peel the root, dice it, and put it in the processor or blender jar with a bit of white vinegar and a pinch each of salt and sugar. Pulse the machine on and off a few times until the root is grated. Do *not* purée it. Store in the refrigerator. Most delis and supermarkets sell refrigerated jars of grated horseradish in vinegar. Gold's horseradish is very hot and very good. Experiment until you find a brand you like. Red horseradish in jars is colored with beet juice. It is fine with gefilte fish, but do not use it as a recipe ingredient.

A NOTE ON PORTION SIZE

T he best delis are famous for two things: the quality of their food and the size of their portions. In this book, the portions are considerably smaller than is strictly traditional. Feel free to adjust them to the appetites of those you feed.

"Following the Rumanian tradition, garlic is used in excess to keep the vampires away; following the Jewish tradition, a dispenser of schmaltz is kept on the table to give the vampires heartburn if they get through the garlic defense."

CALVIN TRILLIN
Alice, Let's Eat, 1978

RENDERED CHICKEN FAT

Rendered chicken fat (schmaltz) is the soul of Eastern European Jewish meat cookery. Because of religious dietary law, orthodox Jews cannot cook or serve meat with butter, cheese, cream, or milk. Pork is forbidden, so that versatile, flavorful animal fat, lard, is strictly out of bounds. As a result, over the centuries chicken fat and, to a lesser extent, other poultry fats have been used for frying, sautéing, flavoring, and enrichment. In a container in your freezer, save the globs of fat and fatty skin that you pull from chickens. When you have acquired a pound or so, thaw it, render it, and store it in the refrigerator. (Some delis and kosher butchers sell frozen 1-pound blocks of chicken fat, ready to be thawed and rendered.) Rendered fat will keep for a week in the refrigerator.

In some recipes vegetable oil can be substituted for chicken fat, but you will be in danger of losing the soul of the dish. Also, keep this in mind: melting chicken fat will fill your kitchen with a luscious, homey aroma that will immediately make all the members of your household feel safe, warm, and loved.

Makes 2 cups

1 pound chicken fat and fatty skin
1 onion, minced

1. Cut the fat and skin into pieces. Put them in a heavy skillet with 1 cup water and the onion and cook over moderate heat. When the water has evaporated and the skin and onion are beginning to brown, turn the heat to low and cook until the fat has completely melted and the skin and onion are deeply browned and crisp.

2. Strain, using a sieve or strainer, the liquid fat into a jar. Cover and refrigerate.

3. Scrape the browned onion and cracklings into a jar. These are called the grebenes and are considered a great delicacy. Use in chopped liver, mashed potatoes, or kasha. The grebenes may also be salted and gobbled like potato chips. Grebenes fans will hover over the pan, ready to snatch them from under your nose.

"In many cases shortening may be substituted [for schmaltz], just as a muskrat coat may be substituted for a mink."
    SARA KASDAN
    Love and Knishes, 1956

BROWNED ONIONS

This is a very important recipe. Use it as a base for other recipes, or to festoon hot dogs, hamburgers, omelets, and skirt steaks. Use the largest, sweetest yellow onions you can get. The trick to making this properly is caramelizing the onions' natural sugar. If the only yellow onions available are not particularly sweet, add a good pinch of sugar in step 3.

The onions must be treated with a great deal of care; it is all too easy for them to burn and become bitter and acrid. First steam them gently in their own juices. This tames them and enables you to sauté them to the proper degree of caramelization.

Makes 2 cups

1 tablespoon vegetable oil
4 tablespoons clarified butter or rendered
    chicken fat (page 11), or 5 tablespoons
    oil
8 cups (about 2 pounds) thinly sliced large
    yellow onions (halve onions before
    slicing)
¼ cup broth or water

1. Heat the oil and butter in a deep, heavy skillet. Toss the onions thoroughly in the hot fat. Cover the skillet and cook over low heat for 10 minutes.

2. Keep the skillet covered, but raise the heat to moderate for 5 minutes.

3. Uncover, raise the heat a bit more, and cook, stirring frequently, until the onions are a deep brown, *almost* burned. As you stir, keep scraping up the browned particles on the bottom of the skillet. The browning time will be anywhere from a half hour to an hour, depending on the moisture and sugar content of the onions and the thickness of your skillet. Never allow the onions to become crisp.

4. When the onions are a deep brown, stir in the broth and bring to a boil. Boil, stirring and scraping up the browned deposits on the skillet, until the liquid cooks away. (This recipe can be doubled or tripled, in which case the browning should be done in a 350° F oven. Spread the onions in a shallow baking dish and bake, stirring occasionally, for an hour or more.)

5. Store in the refrigerator in a covered container and use as needed. They will keep for 1½ weeks.

"But the main standby for flavoring and trimming was the onion. There was no limit to its uses and versatility and there was no meal without it. Sliced, browned, or cooked, it was there."

YURI SUHL
One Foot in America

SOUR CREAM

Sour cream is vital to Eastern European dairy cookery. It garnishes soups, blankets potato pancakes, blintzes, and desserts, and enriches sauces. At many dairy restaurants and nonkosher delis, diners can order large bowls of the thick, tangy cream, garnished with cold chopped raw vegetables, fruit, or—best of all—a steamy-hot boiled potato. When buying sour cream, choose a brand that contains no fillers. Better yet, make your own. It will be silkier, thicker, and creamier than commercial brands.

Heavy cream (not ultrapasteurized)
Cultured buttermilk

1. For every cup of cream, stir in 4 tablespoons buttermilk. With a wire whisk, mix it very well. Pour into a clean glass jar and cover tightly.

2. Allow to stand in a warm part of the kitchen for 2 to 4 days, until it sours and thickens. (The amount of time will depend on the temperature of your kitchen.)

3. Refrigerate and use as needed. It will continue to thicken somewhat in the refrigerator.

TEARS OF JOY

You will weep copious tears while preparing deli recipes. Deli isn't deli without tons of onions. There are countless folk remedies for the problem of onion tears but, alas, they don't work. I have tried to curb my onion sobbing by peeling and slicing them while they were under water, slightly chilled, or partly frozen; I have chopped them near an open window, under an exhaust fan, with a wooden kitchen match clenched firmly between my teeth. Each time, as the tears poured down my cheeks, I was forced to exclaim, "This method (sniff, sniff) does not work!" My twelve-year-old son has come up with the perfect solution. When I start rummaging around in the onion bin, he walks in wearing a gas mask. He has found that swim goggles work well, too.

DELI MUSTARD

For proper deli sandwiches, store-bought mustard just will not do. You need a dark brown, spicy, not too hot, slightly sweet blend to make the most of your homemade breads and fillings.

Makes 1 cup

5 level tablespoons imported dry mustard
¼ cup mustard seeds
1 cup cider vinegar
1 large garlic clove, peeled and crushed
2 tablespoons dark brown sugar
1 teaspoon salt
¼ teaspoon ground ginger
¼ teaspoon ground allspice
¼ teaspoon ground cinnamon
1 to 2 teaspoons clover honey (optional)

1. Whisk together the dry mustard, mustard seeds, and ½ cup warm water in a heavy nonreactive saucepan. Set aside.

2. In a second nonreactive saucepan, combine all the remaining ingredients except the honey. Bring to a boil, reduce the heat, and simmer gently for 5 minutes. Let cool for 2 or 3 minutes. Whisk the spiced vinegar into the mustard.

3. Bring to a simmer and simmer very gently, stirring frequently, for 10 minutes; it should just bubble gently around the edges. With a rubber spatula, scrape the mixture into a bowl. Let stand for 2 hours.

4. Scrape the mustard into the container of a food processor. Process to a grainy purée.

5. Add honey to taste and flick the processor on and off a few times to blend.

6. Scrape the mustard into a jar. Cover and allow to mellow overnight at room temperature. Store in the refrigerator.

MUSTARD

Good mustard is essential to deli food; it enhances and complements the food, stimulates the taste buds, and proclaims the authenticity and good taste of the restaurant. I always begin my judgment of a deli by taking a ceremonial spoonful of mustard from the unmarked glass jar on the table. If it is store-bought, forget it. You may as well leave without so much as inhaling the aroma of a bowl of soup. The best delis have special mustard men who report for duty once a month or so. They slink in after dark and lock themselves in one of the small, mysterious rooms that are invariably found under exemplary delis. They do their alchemy with ground mustard and mustard seed, herbs, spices, and vinegar, and slink away again, leaving a month's supply of the gorgeous condiment. Ask a good deli man for his mustard recipe and he stares in mingled disbelief and horror. Press the point and he makes it quite clear that there are some questions you just don't ask.

MAYONNAISE

Substantial salads are a major part of a deli's menu. Mayonnaise dresses almost all of them. Homemade mayonnaise can be exquisite, but it is wrong for deli salads. For authentic flavor, the mayonnaise must come out of a jar. Not just any jar; only Hellman's will do. Use this homemade mayonnaise as a spread for sandwiches of hard-boiled eggs, turkey, chicken, and onions.

Makes 1 ½ cups

3 egg yolks, at room temperature
Salt and freshly ground pepper to taste
2 teaspoons white wine vinegar
4 teaspoons deli mustard (page 14)
¾ cup olive oil
¾ cup corn oil
1 to 2 tablespoons fresh lemon juice

1. With a wire whisk, in a nonreactive bowl, stir together the egg yolks, salt and pepper, vinegar, and 2 teaspoons mustard.

2. Combine the oils. Add by droplets, whisking very hard. As the mayonnaise begins to thicken, add oil in larger driblets, whisking it in vigorously all the while.

3. When the sauce will absorb no more oil, whisk in the lemon juice and the remaining mustard. Store in the refrigerator.

"In a delicatessen, mustard is like the fine sauce in a French restaurant."
LEO STEINER
Carnegie Delicatessen and Restaurant, 1984

RUSSIAN DRESSING

The classic sandwich spread for Reubens and roasted turkey breast.

Makes 1 cup

½ cup bottled chili sauce
½ cup mayonnaise
1 teaspoon prepared horseradish, squeezed dry
Juice and rind of ½ lemon

Whisk together until smooth.

EGG CREAM

Serves 1

3 tablespoons Fox's U-Bet chocolate syrup
3 tablespoons milk
Seltzer (a siphon bottle is best, but seltzer in
    regular bottles will do)

1. Measure syrup and milk into a 16-ounce soda fountain glass.

2. Squirt or pour in seltzer until the glass is half full. While pouring, stir with a long iced-tea spoon.

3. Increase your stirring speed and squirt hard or pour from a height to produce a frothy, foamy head. Drink immediately.

"The third generation calls it [seltzer] poor man's Perrier, but the first generation still remembers it fondly as the poor man's Champagne."
The American Jewish Almanac, 1980

EGG CREAMS

Egg creams were the *vin ordinaire* of the candy-store set, the wonderful New York nectar that soothed deep thirsts, light hungers, and temporary sorrows. Now that the old-fashioned candy store is almost a thing of the past, egg creams are in danger of vanishing altogether. Every once in a while a nonkosher deli will offer an egg cream on its menu, in an effort to postpone the drink's total extinction. At Sammy's Roumanian Steak House, an ebullient and boisterous bastion of Eastern European Jewish gastronomy on New York's Lower East Side, egg creams are a fact of life. At Sammy's each table holds a cloudy blue siphon bottle of seltzer, right next to the bowl of pickles and the pitcher of rendered chicken fat. A big sign near the door entreats, "No carbonic interplay between customers." When it's time for dessert, the lovably irreverent waiters will plunk a carton of milk and a jar of Fox's U-Bet syrup on the table. Pour in the syrup, splash in the milk, wield the seltzer bottle, stir with abandon, and there you are: the perfect egg cream. It brings tears to the eyes of the terminally nostalgic.

Appetizers

"There were also lots of delicacies such as chopped liver with hard-boiled eggs and onion, which she made herself. She would chop the liver in a wooden bowl with a special chopping knife. It was very simple. She would just go chop-chop-chop at a steady 5-per-second rhythm for half an hour. When I try it, even now as an adult, my arm falls off after 20 seconds."

ISAAC ASIMOV
In Memory Yet Green, 1979

CHOPPED LIVER, 2ND AVENUE DELI

Chopped liver, of course, is a classic deli dish, as an appetizer or a sandwich filling. Everyone has a version. Abe Lebewohl of the 2nd Avenue Deli believes in using just a bit of chicken fat for flavoring. If you use too much, the mixture will be heavy. And be sure not to chop the livers too fine. The texture should remain somewhat grainy.

Makes 2 cups

½ pound calf's liver
½ pound chicken livers
Kosher salt
1 medium onion, coarsely chopped
3½ tablespoons vegetable oil
½ tablespoon rendered chicken fat (page 11)
1 tablespoon finely chopped onion
2 hard-boiled eggs, coarsely chopped
Salt and freshly ground pepper to taste

1. Cover a broiler pan with heavy-duty aluminum foil, shiny side up. Sprinkle the livers with kosher salt on both sides. Broil the chicken livers and then the calf's liver until just done all the way through: about 10 minutes on one side for the chicken livers, 5 minutes on one side for the calf's liver. There is no need to turn the livers over. Chill, then cut into pieces.

2. When the liver has chilled, sauté the coarsely chopped onion slowly in the oil and chicken fat until it is very tender and all its moisture has evaporated. Drain the onion through a sieve, pressing down to extract the fat and oil. Reserve the fat and oil.

3. Scrape the sautéed onion into a wooden chopping bowl. Add the liver, the raw onion, and the eggs. With a hand chopper, chop it all together until it is a cohesive mass, but don't chop it too fine. The texture should be slightly rough. Add enough of the reserved fat to make the chopped liver smooth and unctuous. You will probably find that you need to add all of it. Season to taste with salt and pepper. Scrape it into a crock and chill. Serve with matzoh, pumpernickel (page 57), or rye bread (page 59), or use in sandwiches.

"Even my mother-in-law compliments me on my chopped liver."

Statement on the menu of the 2nd Avenue Deli, 1984

CHOPPED EGGS AND ONIONS

This variation, equally classic, is for those legions who *hate* liver. Use it as you would chopped liver.

Makes 2 cups

2 tablespoons rendered chicken fat (page 11)
1 tablespoon vegetable oil
2 medium onions, finely chopped
6 hard-boiled eggs
1 tablespoon minced raw onion
Salt and freshly ground pepper to taste

1. Heat the fat and oil. Toss in the onions. Cover and steam for 10 minutes. Uncover, raise the heat a bit, and sauté until deeply browned. Drain the onions and reserve the sautéing fat and oil.

2. In a wooden bowl, with a hand chopper, chop the hard-boiled eggs roughly. Add the browned onions and raw onion and chop together. Add about 1½ tablespoons of the reserved fat and oil. Season with salt and pepper. Toss very gently with two wooden spoons. Taste and add more of the fat or more salt and pepper if needed.

3. Scrape into a crock and chill overnight to let the flavors develop. Taste and adjust seasonings before serving.

IT AIN'T CHOPPED LIVER

It was the sculptors' medium that made it an extraordinary artistic event. The medium was brown, malleable, responsive, and very satisfying to work with. Mud? No—chopped liver.

This very odd sculpture festival occurred on October 13, 1976, sponsored by Push Pin Studios in New York. The sculptors chose to depict cartoonish and hilarious subjects (for instance, an angry King Kong crouching atop the Empire State Building; a *zaftig*, emphatically female, naked chicken reclining voluptuously on a bed of greens). New York's 2nd Avenue Deli provided the chopped liver (heavy on the schmaltz). Proprietor Abe Lebewohl also provided separate chopped liver for a buffet, so that hungry bystanders would not be tempted to desecrate the works of art by snitching a taste here and there.

"**A delicate person doesn't eat this food.**"
ABE LEBEWOHL
2nd Avenue Deli, 1984

CHOPPED HERRING

This pungent spread makes a lovely first course. If you do not live near a deli that sells pickled herring fillets, buy jars of pickled herring tidbits or herring in wine sauce. Drain, discard the onions in the jar, and proceed with the recipe.

Makes 2 cups

8 ounces pickled herring fillets, cut into pieces
1 tart apple, peeled, cored, and coarsely chopped
1 slice challah, torn into pieces
1 small onion, coarsely chopped
1 hard-boiled egg, coarsely chopped
¼ teaspoon nutmeg
Juice and rind of 1 lemon
½ teaspoon sugar
Freshly ground pepper to taste

1. Combine the herring, apple, bread, onion, and egg in a wooden chopping bowl. With a hand chopper, chop it all together until it is very fine.

2. Mix in the remaining ingredients. Taste and adjust the seasonings. Scrape into a crock and chill overnight. Bring to room temperature before serving. Serve with matzoh or thin slices of pumpernickel (page 57).

SMOKED FISH MOUSSE

Sophie Goldberg of Goldberg's Deli in Atlanta taught me to add a bit of sable for a deeper flavor.

Makes 1 ¼ cups

1 smoked whitefish (about 4 ounces)
3 ounces sable (smoked cod)
8 ounces cream cheese
1 tablespoon chopped chives
1 tablespoon fresh lemon juice

1. Skin the whitefish. Bone it as follows: open the fish and press it, cut side opened and down, against your work surface. Press down along the backbone. Turn it over and pull the backbone out. Remove any little bones that are left. Discard the head and tail. Discard the skin from the sable. Flake the fish and put it in the food processor. Add the remaining ingredients and process until smooth.

2. Scrape into a serving bowl and smooth with a rubber spatula. Store in the refrigerator. Remove from the refrigerator ½ hour before serving. Serve with matzoh or thin slices of pumpernickel, or with bagels for brunch.

PICKLED LOX IN CREAM SAUCE

I was inspired to develop this recipe after listening to Floridian Lee Levrey reminisce about the legendary Miami Jewish Country Club chef, Pickled Herring Charlie, and his pickled lox with red onions. If you don't make your own lox (page 80), try to find a deli that sells Nova trimmings. It will make this dish much less expensive. For a more delicate (and less traditional) taste, substitute white wine vinegar for the cider vinegar.

Serves 4 to 6

½ pound Nova Scotia or homemade lox
    (page 80), in one piece
4 sweet red onions, cut in half and sliced into
    thin half-moons
½ cup cider vinegar
¼ cup water
1 teaspoon sugar
1 bay leaf
¼ teaspoon whole black peppercorns
¼ teaspoon whole coriander
½ cup sour cream

1. Cut the lox into 1-inch chunks. Toss with the onions in a nonreactive bowl.

2. Combine all the remaining ingredients except the sour cream. Bring to a boil. Let cool thoroughly.

3. Pour over the lox. Cover well with plastic wrap and refrigerate for 48 hours. Uncover and stir occasionally during this time.

4. Drain, reserving the liquid. Put lox and onions in a nonreactive serving dish. Pick out as many of the spices as you can.

5. Beat the sour cream into the reserved liquid. Pour over the lox. Serve with pumpernickel. The dish will keep in the refrigerator for a week.

"Tell an old-timer, waiting on line for her Sunday half pound of lox, that she's eating sashimi and she'll never believe you."
MARK RUSS FEDERMAN
Russ and Daughters, 1984

GEFILTE FISH, RATNER'S

Gefilte fish means stuffed fish, and originally the dish was prepared by stuffing the whole fish skeleton and skin with a fish forcemeat. Later this was changed to fish balls stuffed into a casing of fish skin. I remember having this version as a child, and hating it. Today the dish is presented as a kind of *quenelle*: fish, onion, seasonings, and—usually—matzoh meal, formed into balls and cooked gently in fish stock. The fish balls are served cold, in their jellied broth, with a side of sinus-blasting horseradish. I love this modern version of gefilte fish, and my all-time favorite is served at Ratner's, the venerable and famous dairy restaurant on New York's Lower East Side. Their version is unusual because it contains challah instead of matzoh meal. The recipe is from *Ratner's Meatless Cookbook*.

Serves 8

Fish bones and heads removed from fish
4 carrots, sliced
1 cup sliced celery
½ cup chopped parsnips
1 large onion, sliced
2 tablespoons salt
2 pounds boneless yellow pike
2 pounds boneless carp
2 pounds boneless whitefish
1 large onion
6 slices challah
1 teaspoon white pepper
4 eggs
¼ cup oil
Horseradish

1. In a large pot combine the fish bones and heads, 3 quarts water, carrots, celery, parsnips, sliced onion, and 1 tablespoon salt. Bring to a boil, then reduce the heat and simmer.

2. In a wooden bowl, with a hand chopper, chop the fish with the whole onion and challah until very smooth.

3. Beat in ½ cup water, pepper, the remaining salt, and the eggs and oil.

4. With wet hands, shape 1 cup of the fish mixture into an egg shape. Drop into the simmering fish stock. Repeat with remaining fish mixture.

5. Cover the pot and simmer for 1½ hours. Remove the fish and place in a dish large enough to hold them in one layer. Scatter cooked carrots over and around the fish.

6. Strain the stock and pour it over the fish. Refrigerate. Serve cold with the jellied broth. the carrots, and horseradish.

ENHANCED GEFILTE FISH

In a New Orleans bookshop, I picked up a charming little booklet called *Matzoh Ball Gumbo,* written by the women of the Liberal Synagogue in Baton Rouge. I have used their recipe for gussied-up store-bought gefilte fish many times. It's a great time-saver, and it is special enough to serve to guests.

Makes 12 pieces

1½ tablespoons vegetable oil
1 large onion, cut in half and sliced into thin
    half-moons
3 celery stalks, sliced
½ bell pepper, seeded and sliced
1 medium tomato, peeled and seeded
1 small bunch carrots, peeled and sliced
12 pieces bottled gefilte fish with their jellied
    broth
Juice of ½ lemon
1 teaspoon sugar
Salt and freshly ground pepper to taste
Horseradish

1. Heat the oil in a nonreactive pot. Sauté the onion, celery, and bell pepper until tender and golden but not brown.

2. Add the tomato, carrots, and jellied gefilte fish broth. Season with lemon juice, sugar, and salt and pepper.

3. Bring to a simmer. Simmer until the carrots are almost tender.

4. Add the gefilte fish and simmer for a few more minutes, until the carrots are tender. Let cool, then chill in the refrigerator. Serve with horseradish.

"Gefilte fish is delish. Sturgeon and smoked salmon are sandwiched salubriously. Steaks are noble, and Lindy's cheesecake a headliner."

LAWTON MACKALL
Review of Lindy's, *Knife and Fork in Manhattan,* 1948

CHICKEN FRICASSEE WITH MEATBALLS

I spent a day under Abe Lebewohl's comforting wing at the 2nd Avenue Deli, tasting a vast array of delicacies. This dish is one of his regular menu items. The ingredients are so humble and the cooking method is so simple, yet the results are so outrageously good. The fricassee may be made a day ahead and refrigerated.

Serves 8

½ pound chicken gizzards
½ cup chopped celery
½ cup chopped onions
Chicken broth as needed
1 pound ground chuck
2 garlic cloves, minced
2 tablespoons grated onion
1 slice stale bread, soaked in water and
　　squeezed dry
1 egg
Salt and freshly ground pepper to taste
1 chicken neck
1 carrot, peeled and sliced
6 chicken wings, wing tips removed, cut in
　　two at the joint
1 teaspoon Hungarian paprika

1. Put the gizzards, celery, and chopped onions in a pot. Add water to cover by 1½ inches. Bring to a boil, reduce the heat a bit, and simmer briskly until the gizzards are almost tender, about 1¼ hours, skimming off scum and foam as necessary. If the liquid begins to cook down too much at any time, add a bit of broth.

2. Meanwhile, heat the oven to 350°F. Combine the chuck, garlic, grated onion, bread, egg, and salt and plenty of pepper. Mix together gently and form into balls about ¾ inch in diameter.

3. Spread the meatballs out on a baking sheet. Bake for 10 minutes, until browned and partially cooked through. Set aside.

4. After 1¼ hours, when the gizzards are almost done, add the chicken neck and carrot and simmer briskly for 10 minutes more. Add a bit of broth if necessary.

5. Cut each gizzard in half. Pour the gizzards, neck, vegetables, and their broth into a casserole. Add the wings. Season with more salt and pepper and the paprika. Bring to a simmer on top of the stove. Transfer to the oven and cook, uncovered, for 10 minutes.

6. Add the meatballs and return to the oven for an additional 10 minutes, or until cooked through. Taste and adjust the seasonings.

Soups

"You can teach anyone, Jewish or not, how to make chicken soup, but you can't teach anyone (an ancient ethnic mystery) how to get it up to the temperature of molten lava. A good matzoh ball from such soup does melt in the mouth, but it also hardens again in the stomach. Cases of internal matzoh ball blockage can be cleared by doses of 340-degree chicken soup."

SAM LEVENSON
Saturday Review, March 1980

CHICKEN SOUP

This is the real thing, deli chicken soup, one of the most powerful culinary panaceas of all time. This particular version is served at the Cornucopia deli on New York's Upper East Side. Proprietor Jerry Goldsmith uses his mother Lillian's recipe. He likes to serve the chicken and vegetables in the soup; I prefer to take them out (they have given their all to the broth) and serve the soup with just a bit of dill or parsley, or with the accompaniments suggested at the end of the recipe. Without the dill, it makes an excellent base for other soups. (It's a good idea to save odd chicken parts—wing tips, backs, giblets—in a bag in the freezer. Then, when you make chicken soup, add them for extra strength.)

"Chicken soup...is recommended as an excellent food as well as medication."
MOSES MAIMONIDES,
Twelfth century

Makes 10 cups

1 (3-pound) chicken with giblets (excluding liver)
Any chicken parts you have saved
3 celery stalks
2 carrots
2 parsnips
1 garlic clove, peeled and lightly crushed
2 thin onion slices
⅓ medium boiling potato, peeled
Salt
Freshly ground pepper (use white pepper if you hate black specks in your soup)
Fresh dill

1. Cut the chicken into parts. Clean well: remove pinfeathers and impurities, pull off excess fat, and rinse in warm water. Scrub the celery, carrots, and parsnips, leaving the carrots and parsnips unpeeled. Cut the vegetables into bite-size pieces.

2. Boil the chicken, giblets, and any extra chicken parts in 1 gallon water. After 10 minutes, skim all foam and scum from top. Add the garlic, vegetables, and a little bit of salt (not too much now, or as the soup cooks down it will become much too salty). Reduce the heat so the liquid stays at a steady simmer. Simmer, partially covered, for 1 hour and 10 minutes.

3. Season with salt and pepper to taste. Allow to cool, partially covered. Strain the soup through a fine sieve. Press down on the solids to extract all their goodness. Pour the soup into jars, cover tightly, and refrigerate.

4. Next day, scrape off the fat. The soup will probably have jelled, a sign that you have made a good, gelatin-rich broth. It will liquefy again when heated. Heat. Stir in dill, taste, and adjust the seasonings. Serve piping-hot as is, or with matzoh balls (page 27), kreplach (page 28), kasha (page 48), or noodles.

MATZOH BALLS

Matzoh balls are tender dumplings that are cooked like pasta in boiling salted water and served in rich chicken soup. They may also be served without the soup in shallow bowls, surrounded by sautéed or stewed mushrooms, browned onions, or glazed carrots.

Makes 14

2 eggs, separated
½ cup chicken soup, at room temperature
1½ tablespoons cold rendered chicken fat
    (page 11)
1 cup matzoh meal
Salt and freshly ground pepper to taste

1. With a wire whisk beat the egg whites until foamy. Lightly beat the yolks. Whisk together the whites, yolks, and chicken soup. Thoroughly whisk in the chicken fat. Stir in the matzoh meal. Season generously with salt and pepper. Taste the mixture. It should be peppery and well salted, or else the finished matzoh balls will be insipid. Add more seasoning if necessary. Refrigerate for 1 hour.

2. Remove the mixture from the refrigerator. Roll into walnut-size balls, about 14 in all. Place on a plate and refrigerate until needed (up to 1 hour).

3. One at a time, lower the matzoh balls on a slotted spoon into 5 quarts boiling water. Cover the pot and boil for 30 minutes, until the matzoh balls are expanded, fluffy, and cooked through.

4. Gently remove the matzoh balls with a slotted spoon or a skimmer and put directly in the hot chicken soup. Serve at once.

Note If you must, make the matzoh balls a day ahead of time and refrigerate in the soup. Heat the soup and matzoh balls gently together on the next day. The matzoh balls will be very flavorful from their overnight immersion in the soup, but denser than the day before.

KREPLACH

These tender noodle pockets of chopped meat are the Jewish relatives of Chinese wontons and Italian ravioli. Kneading, rolling, and filling the noodle dough by hand is fun, therapeutic, and easier than many people think. The more adept your noodle technique, the more kreplach you will get per batch of dough. You may get fewer than the maximum amount the first time.

Makes 50

Filling
3 pounds flanken
3 medium onions
1 celery stalk, cut in half
salt
2 tablespoons rendered chicken fat (page 11)
Freshly ground pepper to taste
1 egg, beaten

1. Place the flanken in a saucepan with cold water to cover generously. Bring to a boil. Skim off the scum and foam.

2. Quarter 1 onion and add it to the meat, along with the celery and salt. Cover and simmer briskly for about 1 hour, or until the meat is tender.

3. Drain. Discard the onion and celery. Let the meat cool.

4. Melt the fat in a heavy skillet. Mince the remaining onions. Toss the onions in the hot fat. Cover and steam for 10 minutes. Uncover and sauté until pale golden.

5. Cut the cooled meat into chunks. Discard the bones. In a wooden bowl, with a hand chopper, chop the meat fine. Mix in the onions and their fat. Season with salt and pepper. Stir in the egg.

Dough
2¼ cups unbleached flour
2 eggs, at room temperature
½ teaspoon salt
1 egg, lightly beaten

1. Mound the flour on a work surface. Make a well in the flour. Drop in the eggs and salt. Have 1 cup warm water in a measuring cup on your work surface. With a fork, break the egg yolks. Use the fork to bring flour into the eggs from all sides of the well. As a shaggy dough forms, use your hands to incorporate all the flour into the eggs. Gather the mass together. Sprinkle on some water. Work the mass with your hands as you sprinkle, using approximately ¼ cup water in all. If the mixture gets too wet, sprinkle in a bit of flour; if too dry, sprinkle on some water.

2. When the shaggy mass forms a cohesive dough, knead it thoroughly until it is satiny smooth and very elastic. If at any time it becomes difficult to knead, let it rest for 5 minutes and begin again. When it is very smooth, responsive, and elastic, form it into a ball and cover with an inverted mixing bowl. Let it rest for 30 minutes.

3. Line two baking sheets with wax paper. Flour lightly. Have three damp towels ready.

4. Divide the dough into thirds. Roll each between your hands into a ball. Put one on your work surface. Cover the remaining balls of dough with a damp towel. Use a rolling pin and your hands to roll and stretch the dough into a circle about ⅛ inch thick. At this point the dough should be very elastic and should roll and stretch easily.

5. Use a 3-inch-diameter drinking glass or round cookie cutter to cut circles out of the dough. Gather up any scraps, knead together, and place under the damp towel.

6. Place a generous teaspoon of filling in the center of each circle. Dip your finger in the beaten egg and moisten all around the outer edge of the circle. Fold over into a half-moon shape and press together. Pinch the edges together very well. Place on the wax-paper-covered baking sheet. Cover with a damp towel. Repeat until all the circles are filled, then repeat with the remaining balls of dough. Combine the scraps, knead together, form into a ball, roll out, and cut into circles. Fill and fold as above.

7. To freeze the kreplach, spread on baking sheets, cover with foil, and freeze. When they are solid, transfer to plastic bags. To cook, drop frozen kreplach into boiling chicken soup. (The soup may be diluted with water.

As it boils, the water will evaporate and the broth will regain its strength.) Boil the kreplach for 12 to 15 minutes, until very tender. Serve in deep bowlfuls of the soup, or serve in shallow bowls, moistened with just a bit of soup.

8. To cook kreplach if they have not been frozen, boil in chicken soup for 10 to 12 minutes, or until very tender. Serve as above.

FRIED KREPLACH Film a heavy skillet with vegetable oil. Heat until rippling. Place boiled, drained, and blotted kreplach in one layer in the hot oil. (They should not touch each other or they will steam rather than fry.) Cook until lightly browned and crisp on one side. Turn gently with a spatula. Cook until the second side is browned and crisp.

BEDEVILED KREPLACH

When boiling kreplach, there is always the awful danger of the wrapper's opening, causing the filling to spill into the water, making an unappetizing mess. Old-time cooks believed that you could crimp the wrapper with exquisite care but it would do no good at all if the devil was watching. It was his infernal pleasure to cause the kreplach to burst open as they boiled. The trick was to make the kreplach without attracting the attention of the evil and mysterious one. Of course, if you are making kreplach, you must count them, or how do you know that you have enough? But if you count them, the devil will surely hear. The solution? Count them, but not so the devil notices. Point your finger at each one and firmly say: "Not one, not two, not three . . ."

MUSHROOM BARLEY SOUP

Serves 6

1 ounce dried Polish mushrooms
4 tablespoons rendered chicken fat or butter
2 pounds fresh mushrooms, quartered
2 garlic cloves, peeled and lightly crushed
1 bunch scallions, sliced
4 cups chicken broth or water
½ cup pearl barley
Salt and freshly ground pepper to taste
Sour cream (optional)

1. Rinse the dried mushrooms well under cold running water. Soak them in 2 cups hot water for 2 hours.

2. Melt the fat in a deep heavy pot. Add the fresh mushrooms, garlic, and scallions and stir to coat the mushrooms. Cook, stirring occasionally, for 15 minutes, until the mushrooms exude quite a bit of liquid and turn dark.

3. Strain the soaking water from the dried mushrooms through a cheesecloth-lined sieve or a coffee filter, and reserve. Rinse the soaked mushrooms in cold water and trim off and discard any tough stems. Chop the mushrooms coarsely.

4. Add the soaked mushrooms and their filtered water to the soup pot. Add broth, barley, and salt and pepper. Bring to a boil, reduce the heat, and simmer, covered, for 1½ hours, or until the barley is tender. Taste and adjust the seasonings. Serve piping hot. Pass the sour cream, if desired.

DRIED MUSHROOMS

A longing for the intense taste of the dried *Boletus edulis* of the Old Country was responsible for the establishment, early in the century, of two businesses that continue to flourish today.

More than 110 years ago, a Polish Jew named Aaron Moses Kirsch began selling mushrooms, grown and dried on his family farm, to immigrating countrymen. In the New World, a pot of steaming soup, liberally laced with Kirsch's mushrooms, was a reassuring taste of home. Today, in the South Bronx, Aaron Kirsch's grandson Arthur continues the Kirsch Mushroom Company, dealers in dried mushrooms from all over the world.

On New York's Lower East Side, Mark Russ Federman, proprietor of Russ and Daughters, is upholding the business that began with *his* grandfather. More than eighty years ago Joel Russ, an immigrant from Austria, sold dried Polish mushrooms from a pushcart. He bought his supplies from Aaron Kirsch's son. Today Russ and Daughters, one of the leading food specialty shops in the country, occupies a building located around the corner from the original pushcart site. On weekends, expensive automobiles pull up to the curb and uptown types dash in to purchase exquisite smoked fish and caviar. Mark Federman buys the dried Polish mushrooms he stocks in his shop from Arthur Kirsch. The grandchildren of the original Polish immigrants keep the mushroom business brisk. The culinary tradition of cooking up steaming pots of mushroom-rich soups has spanned the generations.

SPLIT PEA SOUP

Rendered chicken fat is essential to the authentic flavor of this soup. As a change, you might want to substitute garlic croutons (made with cubes of pumpernickel sautéed in garlic-flavored oil) for the knackwurst. Add the croutons at the very last minute.

Serves 6

2 tablespoons rendered chicken fat (page 11)
1 onion, coarsely chopped
1 large carrot, peeled and coarsely chopped
1 large celery stalk, sliced
2 garlic cloves, peeled and lightly crushed
1 cup split peas, washed and picked over
6 cups chicken broth
Salt and freshly ground pepper
6 ounces kosher knackwurst, sliced
    ½ inch thick

1. Heat the fat. Toss in the onion, carrot, and celery. Cover and steam over low heat for 10 minutes.

2. Uncover, raise the heat, and sauté until they are beginning to brown very slightly.

3. Stir in the garlic, split peas, and broth. Season with a bit of salt and a grinding of pepper. Simmer for 1 ½ hours, until the split peas are very tender. Let cool slightly.

4. Purée a little more than half of the soup through a fine sieve. Combine the sieved and unsieved portions. Add the sliced knackwurst. Simmer for 15 minutes, taste for seasoning, and serve. This is delicious on the second day, but it will need to be thinned with a bit of broth.

"There was something delightfully fresh and gay about having a delicatessen supper at eleven at night."

HERMAN WOUK
Marjorie Morningstar, 1955

HOT BEEF AND CABBAGE BORSHT

Serve this splendid Russian Jewish soup with good bread and you have a full meal, capable of sustaining you through bitter winters as well as winters of the soul.

Serves 8 to 10

½ pound fresh sauerkraut (page 46)
2¼ pounds cabbage, cored and trimmed of
    tough, veiny outer leaves
2 tablespoons oil
2 pounds flanken
2 tablespoons rendered chicken fat (page 11)
    or oil
3 large onions, cut in half and sliced
3 garlic cloves, peeled and lightly crushed
1 (1-pound 12-ounce) can tomatoes, un-
    drained and crushed with the hands
2 quarts beef or chicken broth
Salt and freshly ground pepper to taste
4 tablespoons dark brown sugar
4 tablespoons fresh lemon juice

1. Drain the sauerkraut in a colander, rinse well in cold water, and drain again. Squeeze dry.

2. Shred the cabbage, using the slicing disk of a food processor or a chef's knife.

3. Heat the oil in a deep heavy pot. Dry the flanken with paper towels. Brown the meat, a few pieces at a time. Remove to a platter.

4. When all the meat is browned, pour out the oil. Add the chicken fat to the pot and heat. Toss in the onions, cover, and steam over low heat for 10 minutes.

5. Uncover, turn up the heat, and sauté the onions until brown. As they sauté, stir and scrape with a wooden spoon to dislodge the browned bits on the bottom of the pot.

6. Stir in the garlic, tomatoes and juices, and sauerkraut. Return the flanken to the pot, along with any meat juices that have accumulated on the platter. Stir in the stock, a bit of salt, and a few grindings of pepper. Bring to a boil, reduce the heat, cover, and simmer for 1 hour.

7. Stir in the cabbage. Simmer, covered, for an additional hour, or until the meat is meltingly tender.

8. Remove the meat and bones from the soup. Discard the bones and fat. Cut the meat into small pieces and return to the pot. Add the sugar, lemon juice, and more salt and pepper as needed. Taste the soup. It should have a nice balance of sweet and sour. Add more sugar and lemon juice to taste. Serve in deep soup bowls with pumpernickel (page 57) or rye bread (page 59).

COLD BEET BORSHT

This famous soup is a vibrant, glowing crimson. Some delis and dairies like to stir the sour cream right in, turning the borsht a deep pink. This particular beet borsht is my favorite, developed over the years.

Serves 8

10 beets, peeled and coarsely grated
4 tomatoes, peeled, seeded, and chopped
3 leeks, cleaned, trimmed, and chopped
   (see Note)
¼ cup tomato paste
½ cup lemon juice
⅓ cup sugar
Salt to taste
3 eggs at room temperature
Sour cream

1. Combine beets, tomatoes, leeks, and 9 cups water in a heavy nonreactive pot that can be covered. Bring to a boil, reduce the heat, and simmer for 1 hour, partially covered.

2. Add the tomato paste, lemon juice, sugar, and salt. Simmer for an additional ½ hour. Remove from the heat and let stand for a few minutes.

3. Beat the eggs. Beat in some of the hot soup, a little at a time. Then beat the egg mixture back into the soup.

4. Heat gently for a few minutes, stirring constantly, but do not let it boil or even simmer, or the eggs will scramble. Taste carefully and add additional lemon juice, sugar, or salt if necessary. The soup should be tart, but not unpleasantly so.

5. Let cool, and then chill. Top each serving with a dollop of sour cream.

Note To trim leeks, cut off the tip and "beard." Cut off and discard most of the green portion, leaving just 1 inch of green. With a sharp knife, slash through part of the white bulb and up through the remaining green portion. Wash the leeks well under cold running water, holding them apart at the slash to wash away sand. Then chop and proceed with the recipe.

"Wait until you have tasted our borsht tonight, then you'll know what good food is."
SHOLOM ALEICHEM
Tit for Tat, 1946

SCHAV

Sorrel, a deliciously sour, lemony, leafy herb, grows from May to early fall. It is the key ingredient in a kind of green borsht that can hold its own against the best soups of any other cuisine. Some delis serve schav from jars—an abomination. Find a market or herb farm that sells sorrel, or grow it yourself. Made with water, the soup is kosher; with broth, it's not. Either way it's wonderful.

Serves 4 to 6

1 pound sorrel, stripped from its stems and cut into shreds
1 onion, peeled, cut in half, and sliced into paper-thin half-moons
4 cups water or clear, fat-free chicken broth
1½ tablespoons sugar
3 tablespoons lemon juice
Salt to taste
½ cup sour cream, at room temperature
2 eggs, at room temperature
Sour cream
Sliced scallions (green and white parts)
Cucumbers, peeled and seeded
Chopped radishes

1. Combine the sorrel, onion, and water in a nonreactive pot. Bring to a boil, reduce the heat, and simmer for 15 minutes.

2. Add the sugar, lemon juice, and salt, and simmer for 10 to 15 minutes more. Turn off the heat.

3. Beat the sour cream and eggs together. With a whisk, slowly beat 2 cups of the hot soup into the egg-cream mixture. Slowly pour the mixture back into the soup pot, beating vigorously all the while.

4. Taste and add more salt, sugar, or lemon juice, as desired, but remember that this soup should be tart.

5. Chill the soup. Serve it cold, tasting again for seasonings just before serving. Top each bowl of soup with a dollop of sour cream and a sprinkling of scallions, cucumbers, and radishes.

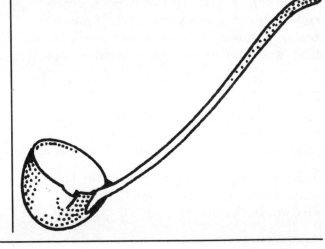

Main Dishes

"And then how about . . . holishkas [stuffed cabbage]—a dish which was probably invented by those alchemists of the middle ages who were trying to make gold out of the baser metals—ground meat and spices wrapped in cabbage leaves and cooked in a sweet and sour raisin sauce, which you eventually sop with a big hunk of rye bread. . . ."

HARRY GOLDEN
Only in America, 1958

STUFFED CABBAGE ON A BED OF SAUERKRAUT

Stuffed cabbage is one of my favorite foods. I had a terrible time trying to choose only one version for this book, so I have settled on two. This one is Hungarian style, and has great delicacy. Do *not* use canned sauerkraut or sauerkraut in plastic pouches. If you do not make your own (page 46) and have no source of barrel sauerkraut nearby, buy the kind that comes in refrigerated jars and contains no added sugar. Even people who think that they hate sauerkraut will fall upon this dish in ecstasy.

Makes 15 to 18 rolls

1 large head cabbage
1 quart fresh sauerkraut
3 tablespoons rendered chicken fat (page 11)
    or vegetable oil
4 onions, chopped
2 garlic cloves, minced
1 tablespoon Hungarian paprika
Salt and freshly ground pepper to taste
1½ pounds veal, ground twice
⅓ cup matzoh meal
2 eggs, lightly beaten
¼ teaspoon dried marjoram
Salt and freshly ground pepper to taste
½ cup tomato purée
½ cup chicken broth, or as needed

1. Cut the core out of the cabbage and pull off the tough outer leaves. Cook the cabbage, in enough boiling water to cover, for 5 minutes, until the cabbage leaves begin to separate and become flexible. As they separate, pull them out carefully with tongs and drain well. Spread the drained leaves on paper towels and cover with additional paper towels to dry.

2. Drain the sauerkraut into a colander. Rinse it very well under cold running water, then drain again and squeeze it as dry as possible. Set aside.

3. Heat the chicken fat in a wide, heavy skillet. Add the onions and garlic, cover, and steam over low heat for 10 minutes. Uncover, raise the heat slightly, and cook until the onions are limp and slightly browned. Stir in the paprika and salt and pepper. Stir over very low heat for about 1 minute, so the paprika loses its raw taste. Set aside.

4. Preheat the oven to 350°F. Put the ground veal in a large bowl. Scrape in half of the onion-paprika mixture. Add the matzoh meal, beaten eggs, marjoram, and salt and pepper. Use your hands or a wooden spoon to mix very well.

5. Add the drained, squeezed sauerkraut to the remaining onion-paprika mixture. Stir it around so the sauerkraut is coated with the paprika. Spread half the mixture on the bottom of a baking dish wide enough to hold the cabbage rolls snugly in one layer.

6. Lay a cabbage leaf, rib side up, on a flat surface. With a sharp knife, pare down the tough rib. Turn the leaf so that it is rib side down. Place some of the meat mixture on the leaf, tuck in the ends, and roll to make a neat parcel. Place seam side down on the sauerkraut in the baking dish. Repeat until all the leaves and stuffing are used. Cover the cabbage rolls with the remaining sauerkraut-onion mixture. Combine the tomato purée and broth and pour over the cabbage. Add

more broth, if necessary, to just barely cover the cabbage rolls. Cover the baking dish with foil and bake for 2 hours.

7. Transfer the cabbage rolls to a dish and set aside. Pour the sauerkraut and sauce into a saucepan, bring to a simmer, and simmer for a few minutes to cook the sauce down a little. Taste and adjust the seasonings.

8. Spread half the sauerkraut and sauce on the bottom of the baking dish. Place the cabbage rolls on it, seam side down, and cover with remaining sauerkraut and sauce. Cover the dish and refrigerate until it is time to reheat it. (It can stay in the refrigerator for several days—the flavor will only improve.)

9. To reheat, bring the dish to room temperature. Bake, covered, in a 350°F oven for 45 minutes to 1 hour, until hot and bubbling.

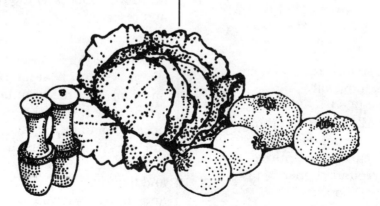

SWEET AND SOUR STUFFED CABBAGE

There are as many versions of this old-fashioned, well-loved dish as there are delis. Sometimes the sweetening agent is brown or white sugar, sometimes honey; and the sour taste may be provided by sour salt (citric acid) or lemon juice. Raisins *must* be in the sauce; here they are paired with dried apricots. This is a festive and beautiful dish, perfect for a party because it can be made several days ahead of time. Serve with kasha or mushroom barley casserole.

Makes 15 to 18 rolls

1 large head or 2 small heads cabbage
5 tablespoons vegetable oil
6 large onions, chopped
1 large (1-pound 12-ounce) can tomatoes, crushed with the hands
1 small (8 ounce) can tomato purée
Salt and freshly ground pepper to taste
3 tablespoons clover honey
¼ cup fresh lemon juice
½ cup raisins
½ cup dried apricots, chopped
¾ pound veal, ground twice
¾ pound beef, ground twice
¼ teaspoon cinnamon
⅛ teaspoon nutmeg
Salt and freshly ground pepper to taste
2 eggs
⅓ cup bread crumbs

1. Cut the core out of the cabbage and pull off the tough outer leaves. Cook the cabbage, in enough boiling water to cover, for 5 minutes, until the cabbage leaves begin to separate and become flexible. As they separate, pull them out carefully with tongs and drain. You should end up with 15 to 18 nice leaves. Spread the drained leaves on paper towels and cover with additional paper towels to drain well. Chop all the remaining cabbage and reserve.

2. To make the sauce, heat 2 tablespoons oil. Toss in one third of the onions. Cover and steam over low heat for 10 minutes. Uncover and cook over medium heat until tender but not browned. Add the tomatoes and their juice, tomato purée, and salt and pepper. Simmer until thickened, about ½ hour. Stir in the honey, lemon juice, raisins, apricots, and half the reserved chopped cabbage. Taste and adjust seasonings. The sauce should have a nice balance of sweet and sour. Set aside.

3. To make the filling, heat the remaining oil. Toss in the remaining onions, cover, and steam for 10 minutes. Uncover and cook until tender and browned. Put the remaining ingredients in a large bowl. Scrape in the onions and the remaining chopped cabbage. Use your hands to mix it all together very well. Fry a tiny piece and taste it. Adjust seasonings.

4. Preheat the oven to 350°F.

5. Choose a baking dish wide enough to hold 15 to 18 cabbage rolls in one layer. Spread a thin layer of sauce on the bottom of the dish.

6. Lay a cabbage leaf, rib side up, on a flat surface. With a sharp knife, pare down the tough rib. Turn the leaf so that it is rib side down. Place some of the meat mixture on the leaf, tuck in the ends, and roll to make a neat parcel. Place seam side down on the sauce in the baking dish. Repeat until all the leaves and stuffing are used. (Form any extra stuffing into small meatballs. Brown on all sides and bake with the cabbage rolls.) Cover the cabbage rolls with the remaining sauce. Cover the baking dish tightly and bake for 2 hours.

To serve, arrange the cabbage rolls on an attractive platter. Pass the sauce separately.

Note This can be prepared several days in advance. The flavor will improve.

EAT, EAT!

In New York dairy and deli restaurants, the waiters contribute as much to the total experience as the food does. Dairy places are home to the classic Jewish grandfather-type waiters. Even if they are relatively young, their hands tremble as they bear the soup to the table, and their eyes beam upon customers with a combination of kindness and exasperation. They fuss at you. They worry that you're eating too much, you're not eating enough, or the combination of foods you have chosen will disagree with you. If you finish your meal nicely, your own mother could not be prouder.

Delis house another sort of classic: The waiters (and sometimes waitresses) with crusty exteriors and hearts of gold. They're tough. They take no nonsense from customers. Try asking for a small portion, or, even worse, for pastrami on white with lettuce and mayo. Try changing tables after your waiter has put you exactly where he wants you. His sneer could turn a person to stone. The responsibility is on the customer. Obey your waiter. While you are under his care, he is the father, you the child. Don't flinch when portions large enough to choke a tyrannosaurus are put in front of you, and do your best to finish it all. Then bask in the glow of pride that floods your soul when he rewards you with a fond glance and a nod of approval.

"Burning is the secret to this kind of cooking!"
Leo Steiner
Carnegie Delicatessen, 1984

ROUMANIAN TENDERLOIN

Skirt steaks are long thin strips of the juiciest, most flavorful beef you have ever tasted. If you can't find them in your market, try a kosher butcher. The steaks should be cooked very quickly over high heat and served smothered with browned onions. Potato kugel is just the right accompaniment. Alternatively, after cooking, the steaks can be cut across the grain into pieces and served on kaiser rolls with the onions.

Freshly ground pepper
Skirt steaks
Salt
Browned onions (page 12)

1. Spread wax paper out on your work surface. Coarsely grind a generous amount of black pepper onto the paper. Press skirt steaks onto the pepper. Grind more pepper onto the top of the steaks. Press in with your hands. Cover with more wax paper. Let stand at room temperature for ½ hour.

2. Heat a well-seasoned cast-iron skillet until very hot. Salt the skirt steaks on both sides. Cut steaks into a size that will fit into the skillet. Put as many steaks into the hot skillet as will fit without touching each other. Cook over high heat on one side for 2 to 3 minutes, turn with tongs and cook on the other side for 2 to 3 minutes. At this point, the steaks should be nice and brown on the outside and juicy and rare within. Remove with tongs to a platter. Let sit for 3 minutes. Serve with heaps of browned onions.

SAMMY'S ROUMANIAN TENDERLOIN At Sammy's Roumanian Steak House in New York, skirt steaks are broiled for 3 minutes on each side and then rubbed with a paste of pounded garlic, salt, and oil.

"...cholent that had been in the oven all night—and you know what that smells like when you take it out of the oven. And what it tastes like. Our visitor could not find words to praise it."

SHOLOM ALEICHEM
Tit for Tat, 1946

CHOLENT 2ND AVENUE DELI

Cholent is a traditional Sabbath-day dish of dried beans, potatoes, fat meat, and onions. It is of the same genre as French cassoulet and New England baked beans. In the hands of some cooks, cholent emerges as an indigestible mass that smites the diner's stomach much as David's stone smote Goliath. Abe Lebewohl's version is substantial but not frighteningly so, if you exercise caution in portion control; a little bit goes a long way. The meltingly tender meat and the deeply flavored, almost creamy beans and potatoes are deeply satisfying. It doesn't pay to make small amounts of cholent. Make a large batch and freeze it in small containers. During a snowstorm, it's great to have a supply of this warming stuff stashed away. It will be necessary to thin the mixture with broth or water when reheating.

Put cholent in the oven at night before you go to bed. You will awaken to the most tantalizing smell imaginable.

Makes 12 cups

1 cup dried lima beans
1 cup dried pinto beans
3 pounds flanken
3 boiling potatoes, peeled and quartered
4 large onions, chopped
Salt and freshly ground pepper to taste

1. Preheat the oven to 200°F.

2. Rinse the dried beans and pick over them for loose stones or dirt.

3. Choose a large, widemouthed casserole. Layer in half of each type of bean, the flanken, the potatoes, the onions, and the remaining beans. Pour in water to cover by 2 inches. Season with salt and a generous amount of pepper. Bring to a boil on the top of the stove. Skim off foam and scum.

4. Bake, uncovered, for 16 to 17 hours. As it cooks a crust will form on top. In the morning, push the crust into the cholent with a wide spatula. Repeat every few hours. When the mixture is thick but not cementlike and the beans are creamy, the cholent is done. Adjust the seasonings.

"The French have cassoulet, we have cholent."
Sign, 2nd Avenue Deli, 1984

BOB GOODMAN'S SWEET AND SOUR BRISKET

Bob Goodman is the proprietor of the Ess Gezunt Deli in Atlanta. The ingredients in his recipe are simple, yet the results are quite spectacular. After baking, the sauce in the baking pan is suave and thick, bearing little resemblance to the original ingredients. The brisket may be prepared a few days in advance. Slice the meat and refrigerate the slices in the sauce. Next day, scrape off any hardened fat and discard. Then heat and serve.

Serves 4 to 6

2 large onions, coarsely chopped
10 garlic cloves, peeled and left whole
1 first-cut beef brisket (about 3½ pounds),
    trimmed of all fat except a thin layer
    on top
Salt and freshly ground pepper to taste
½ cup unsulfured molasses
Juice of 1 large lemon
¾ cup catsup

1. Preheat the oven to 350°F.

2. Put the onions and garlic cloves on the bottom of a shallow baking dish. Cover with ½ cup water. Put the brisket on the onions, and salt and pepper it lightly.

3. Pour the molasses over the meat, pour on the lemon juice, and cover with catsup. Seal the baking dish very well with heavy-duty foil. No steam must escape.

4. Bake for ½ hour. Turn the heat down to 250°F and bake for an additional 2½ hours, or until the meat is very tender. Slice across the grain, and serve with the sauce.

"When I looked at the [menu] I groaned aloud. Was it possible, I thought, that any human being could eat a meal of such length and live?"

LT. COL. NEWNHAN-DAVIS
Review of Goldstein's
The Gourmet's Guide to London, 1914

Vegetables and Side Dishes

"Oh the ecstasy, as teeth snapped through firm
but tender skin to the cool, spicy interior that
slowly, juicily released its counterpointed
flavors of hot peppers, garlic, dill, the piny
bay leaves and exotic mustard seeds and the
faintly winy-cidery tang of the pickling
liquid...."

MIMI SHERATON
on biting into a pickle
From My Mother's Kitchen, 1979

DILL PICKLES

In a real deli, you begin feasting on wonderful things even before you place your order. Overflowing crocks of gorgeous, garlic-scented dill pickles sit on every table, just waiting to be plundered. It is ridiculously easy to make deli pickles at home. The sense of accomplishment on tasting your own first home-cured pickle is almost as intense as on tasting your own first home-baked bread. You may fiddle with the herbs and spices to taste, but *do not* fiddle with the amounts of salt and water; they are essential to the fermenting process. Use small kirbies only, large ones are too seedy. In large cucumbers, the seeds tend to expand and sometimes explode within the pickle, resulting in a pickle that is pulpy or even hollow inside.

Makes 25

¾ cup kosher salt
25 small kirbies (unwaxed pickling
    cucumbers)
15 whole garlic cloves, unpeeled and lightly
    crushed
1 generous bunch fresh dill
3 bay leaves
1 teaspoon coriander seeds
1 teaspoon dill seeds
1 teaspoon whole black peppercorns
1 teaspoon mustard seeds

1. Add the salt to 1 gallon of water and bring to a boil. Let cool thoroughly.

2. Choose a clean widemouthed crock, large enough to hold the cucumbers, with room for the brine to cover them by 2 inches. Wash and scrub the cucumbers very well. They must be firm and unblemished. Put the cucumbers, garlic, and dill in the crock. Add the spices.

3. Pour the thoroughly cooled brine over the cucumbers in the crock. The brine should cover the cucumbers by 2 inches. Place a clean plate on the cucumbers and set a weight on it to keep the cucumbers submerged. (A coffee mug filled almost to the top with water makes a perfect weight.) The cucumbers *must* remain completely submerged in the brine. Drape a double-thick veil of cheesecloth over the crock, to keep the dust out. Place in a cool corner of the kitchen.

4. Check the crock every day and skim off any foam or scum. As the days pass, the winy, pickly, spicy smell wafting from the crock will drive all resident pickle lovers into a state of frenzy. Be patient. In approximately 4 days (it depends on the temperature of your kitchen) the pickles will be half sour.

Fish one out with tongs and cut into it to see. If you like half sours, take some out and put them in a clean jar. Pour in enough of the brine to cover them. Put in some of the dill branches and garlic as well. Cover tightly and refrigerate. (They will continue to pickle, but much more slowly.) Reweight the remaining pickles. Check every day. In approximately 10 days they will be completely sour.

As they reach the point that satisfies various members of your household, pull them out, put them in jars with brine, dill, and garlic, and refrigerate.

PICKLED GREEN TOMATOES They are made in exactly the same way as cucumber pickles, except the tomatoes must be pricked in several places with the tines of a fork. Use only hard, thoroughly green tomatoes.

ROASTED ROUMANIAN PEPPERS

At Sammy's Roumanian Steak House in New York City, a big dish of roasted peppers in a secret solution of vinegar, water, and sugar is placed on every table, next to the bowls of pickled cucumbers and tomatoes, the siphon seltzer bottle, and the chicken fat dispenser. Burning the peppers over a flame is lots of fun. Don't worry if you are not able to remove every bit of blackened skin from the peppers. Even at Sammy's, each pepper has a tiny black shred here and there.

6 large bell peppers: red, green, and yellow
5 large garlic cloves, peeled and crushed
Salt
⅔ cup olive oil

1. To roast the peppers, place them directly on the flame of a gas stove. As the peppers blacken and char, turn them with tongs. When they are completely blackened, enclose them in a paper bag for 15 minutes. Remove and scrape off skin with a table knife or your fingers. Cut the peppers in quarters and remove the seeds and ribs. Lacking a gas stove, place peppers on a baking sheet in a 450° F oven. Turn with tongs every 5 minutes or so. When the peppers are blackened, proceed as above.

2. Put the peppers and garlic in a shallow bowl. Sprinkle on salt to taste and pour in the oil. Cover with plastic wrap and refrigerate for at least 2 hours. It may stay in the refrigerator for 2 to 3 days before serving. Leave out for 15 minutes to warm up slightly before serving.

HOME-CURED SAUERKRAUT

Don't think about the limp, horrid, smelly stuff that comes in cans. Fresh sauerkraut is crisp, pungently sour, but not offensively so, and incredibly good. It is the crowning glory of a hot dog and the key ingredient in Hungarian stuffed cabbage. Sauerkraut fans love it eaten straight out of the jar. And remember, fresh sauerkraut juice is reputed to be just the thing for a recalcitrant hangover.

Firm unblemished heads of white cabbage
Uniodized table salt

1. Remove and discard the tough, dark outer leaves from the cabbage heads. Core the cabbage. Cut into quarters.

2. Weigh the cabbage. Measure out 2 level teaspoons of salt for every pound of cabbage.

3. On the slicing disk of a food processor or with a sharp chef's knife cut the cabbage into long thin shreds.

4. Put a layer of cabbage in a very large nonreactive bowl and sprinkle with a bit of salt. Continue layering cabbage and salt until you have used it all. With your hands, toss the cabbage thoroughly until it begins to wilt and release a good quantity of liquid.

5. Transfer the cabbage and all its liquid to a clean nonreactive crock. Press the cabbage down firmly with your fist. Keep pressing and pushing down until the cabbage liquid just covers the surface.

6. Place 1 large plastic food storage bag inside another. Fill the inner bag with 1 quart of water. Carefully place the double bag on top of the cabbage in the crock. Slowly pour more water into the inner bag until the bags spread out enough to completely cover the surface of the cabbage. Tie the bags securely closed. This acts as a weight and keeps air away from the cabbage. Drape a length of cheesecloth over the crock.

7. Place in a quiet corner. The room temperature should be 65° to 72° F. In 6 to 8 days the sauerkraut will be ready. (Toward the middle of the week, your crock may be quite smelly. Don't worry—it's all part of the fermentation process.)

8. When the sauerkraut is done, transfer it and its delicious juices to clean jars. Cover well and store in the refrigerator. It will keep for months.

SAVORY LOKSHEN KUGEL

Lokshen kugel is noodle pudding. There are countless versions of such kugels, both sweet and savory. Either way, they are meant to be served with the main dish. I prefer to serve sweet kugels as dessert (page 90).

Serves 8

½ pound wide egg noodles
2 cups thinly sliced scallions (green and white part)
4 garlic cloves, peeled and crushed
¼ pound butter, melted
4 eggs
1 pound creamed cottage cheese, at room temperature
1 cup sour cream, at room temperature
Salt and freshly ground pepper to taste
1½ cups grated münster cheese
¼ cup bread crumbs
¼ teaspoon Hungarian paprika

1. Preheat the oven to 350° F.

2. Cook the noodles according to package directions. Drain in a colander, rinse under running water, and stir with your hands to separate them.

3. While the noodles are cooking, sauté the scallions and garlic in melted butter until limp and fragrant but not at all browned. When the noodles are drained and rinsed, toss them thoroughly with the butter mixture.

4. Beat the eggs. Beat in the cottage cheese, sour cream, and salt and pepper. Stir in the noodle mixture. Taste and adjust the seasonings. It should be quite peppery and well salted. Pour into a 9 x 13-inch oval glass baking dish.

5. Sprinkle evenly with the cheese, and sprinkle the bread crumbs over the whole thing. Dust evenly with paprika. Bake for approximately 40 minutes, until the kugel is puffed, set, and golden on top.

"...that's the way the kugel crumbles. But even a crumbled kugel is no tragedy. The delicacy... is known as the perfect food, because if it sticks together, you have a marvelous dish; and if it doesn't stick together, you have marvelous ingredients."
ISRAEL SHENKER
Noshing Is Sacred, 1979

KASHA

Kasha is buckwheat groats, available in boxes from many delis, health food stores, and some supermarkets. It makes a nutty brown pilaf, excellent served as an accompaniment to roasted brisket or other dishes with lots of rich gravy. Kasha is also splendid in chicken soup. The recipe may be multiplied as many times as needed.

Makes 4 cups

1 egg, lightly beaten
1 cup kasha, coarse or whole
2 cups chicken broth, brought to a rolling
　　boil
Salt and freshly ground pepper to taste

1. Stir the egg into the kasha. Mix until the kasha grains are well coated with egg.

2. Heat a large, heavy skillet. Stir the kasha in the skillet over moderate heat until each grain is dry and separate. It will give off a delicious toasty odor. This should take about 5 minutes. Scrape the kasha into a large pot that can be covered.

3. Add the boiling broth and salt and pepper. Stir a few times.

4. Cover the pot and simmer over lowest heat for 30 minutes. Turn off the heat, remove the cover, and drape a towel over the pot. Recover and let stand for about 5 to 10 minutes, until all the liquid is absorbed and each grain of kasha is separate.

VARIATIONS Add sautéed onions and mushrooms to the cooked kasha.

Toss chopped walnuts or pecans or whole pine nuts into the cooked kasha.

When preparing kasha, use the filtered soaking water from Polish dried mushrooms in place of half the chicken broth. After the kasha is cooked, toss in the soaked and chopped mushrooms. (Sauté them in a bit of butter, oil, or chicken fat first.)

KASHA VARNISHKES

The combination of noodles, kasha, and burned onions, sautéed in chicken fat, is a beloved deli classic of Polish and Russian Jewish origin. With trepidation I served a big bowl of it to a group of friends who had no experience whatsoever with New York deli culinary tradition. I worried that they would scrutinize the brown-flecked white noodles with disdain, turn away with noses in the air, and refuse to have any part of such an ethnic concoction. On the contrary, they loved it and polished off every morsel, and each guest requested a copy of the recipe.

Serves 4 to 6

2 tablespoons rendered chicken fat (page 11)
1 tablespoon vegetable oil
1 large onion, coarsely chopped
2 cups cooked kasha (previous recipe)
2 cups cooked bow-tie noodles

1. Heat the chicken fat and oil in a wide, heavy skillet. Toss in the onion, cover, and steam for 10 minutes. Uncover and sauté the onion slowly until dark brown, almost burned.

2. Toss in the kasha and noodles. Keep tossing and turning the mixture in the hot fat until everything is thoroughly hot. Scrape into a serving dish and serve at once.

POTATO PIROGEN

These are, essentially, potato kreplach. Noodle dough filled with mashed potatoes may sound like a bit much, but of all the pasta dishes in the world, this is the best.

Makes about 50

Noodle dough (see kreplach recipe, page 28)
½ recipe Potato filling (page 51)
Melted butter

1. Using a 3-inch-diameter drinking glass or cookie cutter, cut out circles of dough according to directions in the kreplach recipe. Fill with a generous spoonful of the potato mixture. Fold and pinch according to kreplach directions.

2. Boil pirogen in a large pot of salted water for approximately 10 minutes, or until very tender. Drain and serve in bowls with melted butter. (Sour cream is traditional too, but melted butter is better.)

LITTLE POTATO KNISHES

Knishes come in many forms. The outer wrapper may be made of a crêpe, yeast dough, baking powder dough, or flaky pastry, and the filling may be potato, kasha, ground beef, or chicken livers. I refuse to consider any kind of knish except potato in flaky pastry. This recipe will produce what I consider to be the world's most perfect potato knish, small, almost dainty; each bite fills the mouth with an intense essence of potato and onion. The only problem is that people eat far too many. Once they start, they can't seem to stop.

Makes 48

8 tablespoons (1 stick) cold butter or
    margarine
8 tablespoons solid vegetable shortening
3 cups unbleached flour
½ teaspoon salt
Potato filling (recipe follows)
2 egg yolks, lightly beaten with 2 tablespoons
    water

1. Cut the butter into pieces and put on a plate. Spoon the vegetable shortening onto the same plate. Pour ice water into a glass measuring cup. Put both the plate and the measuring cup in the freezer.

2. Measure out the flour and salt. Sift them together into a bowl. Remove the plate and cup from the freezer.

3. Your hands must be cool and dry. Scrape the butter and shortening into the flour. Using the tips of your fingers and thumbs, rub the fat into the flour until the mixture turns into coarse, oatmeal-like flakes. Lightly rub the flakes with your fingertips until they break up into small particles. Work lightly and very quickly; the mixture must not become oily.

4. Sprinkle in 6 tablespoons ice water, one at a time. Combine the water with the flour-fat mixture using your fingertips. Cup your hands and gather up the dough into a cohesive mass. If it doesn't cohere, sprinkle in more ice water, droplet by droplet, until it does. Cup hands and form into a ball.

5. Dust the ball very lightly with flour, wrap in plastic wrap, and chill for at least 1 hour. (It can stay in the refrigerator for 3 days or the freezer for 3 months. Thaw in the refrigerator.)

6. Remove the dough from the refrigerator. Divide it in quarters; wrap three quarters and return to refrigerator. Have a small bowl of water ready near your work surface.

7. Flatten the piece of dough. Lightly flour your work surface, the top of the dough, and the rolling pin. Roll dough out into a rectangle about ⅛ inch thick, 10 inches wide, and 16 inches long. Always roll from center out to the edges.

8. Cut the dough lengthwise in half. Place one eighth of the filling in a line down the center of each strip. Use a long metal spatula to help fold the long ends in to cover the filling. Moisten the edges first and then press together so the dough adheres. Use the spatula to turn the filled strips of dough seam side down. Cut each strip into 6 equal pieces. Do not pinch the ends closed. Brush the tops with the egg yolk mixture. Place on an ungreased baking sheet and refrigerate while you repeat with the remaining dough. When all the dough and filling are used, refrigerate for 15 minutes to an hour.

9. Preheat the oven to 425° F. Bake the knishes for 15 to 20 minutes, or until golden. With a spatula, remove to a rack, let stand for 5 minutes, and serve.

Filling
5 tablespoons butter or margarine
4 tablespoons vegetable oil
4 large onions, coarsely chopped
6 medium baking potatoes, peeled and
  quartered
Salt and freshly ground pepper to taste

1. Heat the butter and oil in a heavy skillet. Toss in the onions, cover, and steam over low heat for 10 minutes. Uncover and sauté until the onions are deeply browned.

2. Put the potatoes in a pot filled with cold water to cover generously. Bring to a boil. Boil for approximately 25 minutes, until very tender. Drain, return to the pot, and toss over low heat until dry.

3. With an old-fashioned potato masher, mash the potatoes in the pot until they are very smooth. Scrape in the onions and all their sautéeing fat and oil. Season generously with salt and pepper. With a wooden spoon, beat the onions and potatoes together. Taste and grind in more pepper if necessary; the mixture should be quite peppery. Cool thoroughly before using.

POTATO KUGEL Make any amount of potato filling. Stir in 1 egg per 2 cups of potato mixture. Spread in a shallow baking dish. Bake at 400° F for 35 to 45 minutes, until golden and crusty on top. Rendered chicken fat (page 11) may be substituted for the butter, if desired.

POTATO BLINTZES Make blintz wrappers (page 84) but omit the orange liqueur. Fill with the potato mixture combined with 2 beaten eggs. Sauté in a small amount of oil or clarified butter until golden brown.

LATKES (POTATO PANCAKES)

Forget the food processor for the time being. Invaluable as that machine is, it won't work here. The secret of these spectacular potato pancakes is the use of the *reeb eisel* (grater). The potatoes must be grated into *long* strips. The pancakes must be fried and immediately served, making the cook a temporary slave to the stove, but the results are worth it.

Serves 6

6 medium baking potatoes
2 eggs
1 onion
1½ teaspoons salt
½ cup unbleached flour
Oil or clarified butter
Sour cream or applesauce

1. Scrub the potatoes. (It is not necessary to peel them.) Grate them in long strips (use the large holes on a four-sided grater) into a bowl of cold water.

2. Beat the eggs in a bowl. Grate the onion into the beaten eggs. Stir in the salt and flour.

3. Drain the potatoes very well, squeezing out all excess moisture. Stir together the potatoes and the egg-flour mixture.

4. Pour oil to about ½ inch deep in a wide, heavy skillet, and heat until hot but not smoking. Drop the potato mixture into the hot oil by the heaping tablespoon. Flatten each dollop of batter into a flat pancake. Fry on each side until golden brown and crisp. Drain on paper towels. Serve at once with sour cream or applesauce.

MUSHROOM BARLEY CASSEROLE

This deli standby is excellent with brisket or stuffed cabbage. The vivid flavor of the Polish mushrooms and their soaking liquid make the casserole extraordinarily tasty.

Serves 6

1 ounce dried Polish mushrooms
2 tablespoons rendered chicken fat (page 11) or oil
1 medium onion, chopped
¼ pound small fresh mushrooms, quartered
1 cup medium pearl barley
2 cups chicken broth
Salt and freshly ground pepper to taste

1. Rinse the dried mushrooms well under cold tap water. Soak in hot water to cover generously for 2 hours. Strain the water though a cheesecloth-lined sieve or a coffee filter and reserve. Rinse the mushrooms under running cold tap water. Trim off and discard any tough stems. Chop the mushrooms coarsely.

2. Preheat the oven to 350° F.

3. Heat the chicken fat in a 2-quart casserole. Toss in the onion. Cover and steam for 10 minutes. Uncover and sauté slowly until lightly browned. Toss in the fresh mushrooms. Sauté until tender. Add the chopped Polish mushrooms and the barley. Stir so that everything is well combined.

4. Pour in the stock and ¼ cup of the reserved mushroom liquid. (Save the remainder for soups or sauces.) Season with salt and pepper. Bring to a boil, cover, and put in the oven.

5. Cook for 50 to 60 minutes, or until the barley is tender and the liquid is absorbed. Uncover, drape a kitchen towel over the pot, re-cover over the towel, and let stand for 10 minutes.

"I have only vague memories of Polish delicacies, but I can almost taste the strong flavor and aroma of Polish mushrooms to this day."

HELEN NASH
Kosher Cuisine, 1984

53

CARROTS GLAZED IN CREAM SODA

"Crisp-tender," that sought-after holy grail of nouvelle vegetable cookery, is a deli no-no. It is a basic rule of deli gastronomy that vegetables be overcooked. Fortunately, carrots take to overcooking as a duck takes to water. Carrots also take extremely well to sweetening, another deli culinary predilection. The French cook carrots in sparkling mineral water. Why not, I asked myself, cook carrots in cream soda, that most classic of deli beverages? The results were even better than I expected: sweet but not overly so, vanilla-scented and tender.

Serves 4 to 6

2 pounds carrots, peeled and sliced
12 ounces cream soda
Salt and freshly ground pepper to taste
1 tablespoon dark brown sugar
Juice of ½ lemon

1. Preheat the oven to 400° F.

2. Put the carrots in a baking dish that can work on top of the stove as well as in the oven. Pour in the soda, season with salt and pepper, and sprinkle with sugar. Cover tightly. Bake for 40 minutes.

3. Place the dish on top of stove. Squeeze in the lemon juice. Bring to a boil. Boil, stirring constantly, until the liquid is almost completely cooked away and carrots are lightly glazed.

Breads

"And, on Saturdays, of course, we had a braided egg-bread called 'khalleh,' which was to ordinary bread what diamonds are to rhinestones."

ISAAC ASIMOV
In Memory Yet Green, 1979

55

CHALLAH

What a beautiful bread this is! It is the famous brioche-like Jewish Sabbath bread—excellent for sandwiches, as French toast, and to sop up rich sauces. It may be braided or formed into a spiral; both are traditional.

Makes 1 monumental loaf

3 packages dried yeast
2½ cups warm water (100° to 115° F)
2 tablespoons honey
1 tablespoon kosher salt
¼ cup vegetable oil
5 to 7 cups unbleached white flour
3 eggs
1 egg yolk, mixed with 1 teaspoon water
Poppy seeds

1. Combine the yeast and water in a large bowl.

2. Stir in the honey, salt, oil, 2 cups of flour, and the eggs. Stir with a whisk.

3. Beat in the remaining flour, 1 cup at a time. Switch from the whisk to a wooden spoon as the dough gets stiffer.

4. Turn the dough out onto a floured surface and knead for about 15 minutes, until smooth, satiny, and very lively. This is a very responsive dough. It is easy to work with, and feels about as smooth and soft as a baby's tushy. The dough has been kneaded sufficiently when two lightly poked finger holes spring back. Let the dough rest, covered, while you wash, dry, and oil the large bowl.

5. Form the dough into a ball and place it in the bowl. Turn it so that it is coated with oil. Cover with a clean kitchen towel or plastic wrap and place it in a warm, draft-free place until the dough has doubled in bulk, about 1½ hours. To check for proper rising, gently poke two holes in risen dough and leave for 5 minutes. If the holes remain, the dough is ready.

6. Flour your fist and punch down the dough. Turn out and knead a few times. Then let it rest, covered, for a few minutes. Grease a large baking sheet.

7. Divide the dough into two equal parts. Set one part aside, covered. Divide the remaining piece into three equal parts. Gently pull, roll, and stretch each piece into a thick rope. Starting in the middle, braid the ropes, first down one end, then the other. Pinch the ends together and center the braid on the greased sheet. Divide the remaining piece of dough into four equal parts. Set one piece aside, covered. Form the three pieces into ropes and braid as before, but this braid should be smaller than the first. Set the second braid securely on top of first braid. Pinch the braids together. Pull and stretch the last piece of dough into a short fat rope. Twist it several times. Place it on top of the second braid.

Pinch the dough together so that it doesn't fall off. Cover the entire loaf lightly with a clean dry cloth. Place in a warm, draft-free place to double in bulk, about ½ hour.

8. Preheat the oven to 400°F. Mix the egg yolk and water in a small bowl.

9. When the loaf has risen, brush it with the egg yolk glaze and sprinkle liberally with poppy seeds. Bake for 45 minutes to 1 hour. It is done when it is golden, and a knuckle thump on the bottom produces a hollow sound. Also, a skewer inserted into the loaf will emerge clean. This bread is delicious right out of the oven. Be careful or it will vanish before it even cools.

Note For an alternative (and much easier to execute) shape, do not braid the risen punched-down dough. Instead, gently pull, stretch, and roll all of the dough into a long thick rope. Coil the rope into a large, snail-like spiral. Put the spiral on the oiled pan and continue with the recipe as written.

PUMPERNICKEL

A peasant bread of interesting texture and dark color, pumpernickel is very good for sandwiches. It is also quite good with appetizers such as chopped liver, chopped herring, and lox in cream sauce.

WHAT'S IN A NAME?

The legend is as follows: A horseman (perhaps even Napoleon) paused for refreshment in a small Eastern European town. He wearily dismounted from his trusty horse, Nicole, and looked around for sustenance. A helpful peasant offered him some coarse black bread. The fastidious horseman took one look at the rustic stuff and turned away. "*Bon pour Nicole,*" he sniffed disdainfully (good for my horse). And so pumpernickel was given the name that has stuck with it ever since.

Makes 3 large loaves

1½ cups unbleached white flour
1½ cups whole-wheat flour
2 cups rye flour
½ cup whole bran cereal
½ cup yellow cornmeal
½ cup wheat germ
1 tablespoon unsweetened cocoa
1 tablespoon instant coffee
2 tablespoons kosher salt
1 tablespoon caraway or fennel seeds
1 cup mashed potatoes (1 medium potato)
4 tablespoons butter or margarine
2 packages dried yeast
3½ cups warm water (100° to 115°F)
½ cup molasses
Up to 7 cups additional unbleached white flour
Cornmeal
1 egg

1. Combine the first twelve ingredients in a large bowl.

2. Combine the yeast and warm water in another large bowl. Stir with a fork or small whisk. Add the molasses. Stir the flour mixture into the liquid, 1 cup at a time.

3. Beat the mixture well with a wooden spoon. Beat in enough additional white flour to form a soft, shaggy dough (2 to 3 cups more).

4. Flour a work surface. Turn out the dough and begin kneading. Knead in more white flour to produce a smooth, nonsticky dough (3 to 4 cups more). Knead vigorously for about 20 minutes, until the dough is smooth and lively. It is kneaded sufficiently when a lightly poked finger depression in the dough springs back. Let the dough rest, covered, while you wash, dry, and oil the large bowl.

5. Knead the dough a few more turns. Form it into a ball and place it in the oiled bowl; turn it to cover with oil. Cover the bowl with plastic wrap or a clean kitchen towel and place in a warm, draft-free place until the dough has doubled in bulk. This will take about 1½ hours. When you think it is ready, gently poke two holes in the risen dough and cover it again for about 5 minutes. If the holes remain, the dough has risen sufficiently.

6. Flour your fist and punch down the dough. Turn it out and knead a few times and then let it rest, covered, for 5 minutes.

7. Cut the dough into three equal pieces. Shape each piece into a plump round loaf.

Sprinkle a large baking sheet or two smaller ones with cornmeal. Place the balls of dough on the sheets. Leave plenty of room around them, for they will expand considerably. Cover with a towel or plastic wrap and place in a warm, draft-free place until they have doubled in bulk, 40 to 45 minutes.

8. Preheat the oven to 375°F. Beat the egg with 1 tablespoon water in a small bowl.

9. When the loaves have risen, brush them with the egg glaze. Bake for 1 hour or more, until done. They are done when they emit a hollow sound when thumped on the bottom with the knuckles. Also, a thin skewer inserted all the way into the loaf will come out clean. Let the loaves cool on wire racks.

ONION SANDWICHES

An onion sandwich (particularly the second version) is a bracing experience. After consuming the second version, you will light up the room with an incandescent onion glow every time you exhale, but for an onion lover, it's worth it.

Spread slices of challah with a bit of mayonnaise. Sprinkle with parsley. Place a thin layer of sliced onion on one slice of challah. Top with a second slice of challah and press together. Eat blissfully.

For a more authentic and much more robust sandwich, use crusty rye bread, spread it with solidified rendered chicken fat, sprinkle with kosher salt, and use thick slices of strong onion. Eat bravely.

RYE BREAD

It is impossible to exactly reproduce bakery breads at home. Bakery equipment and ingredients are very different from those available for home use. But you can—with certain little tricks—produce excellent breads, often even better than what you can buy at many bakeries. Here, the use of mashed potatoes produces a tender moist crumb, water brushed on the unbaked loaf produces the hard crust that is so essential to deli rye, and cornmeal on the baking sheet results in a properly crunchy bottom. This is a sensational sandwich bread.

Makes 1 large loaf

1 package dried yeast
2½ cups warm water (100° to 115°F)
2 tablespoons kosher salt
1 tablespoon caraway seeds
3 cups rye flour
1 cup mashed potatoes (1 medium potato)
5 to 6 cups unbleached white flour
Cornmeal

1. Combine the yeast with warm water in a large bowl. Stir with a fork or small whisk. Add the salt and caraway seeds. Stir in rye flour, 1 cup at a time, the potatoes, and the white flour, 1 cup at a time, until a soft dough is formed.

2. Turn the dough out onto a floured surface. Knead vigorously for 20 to 25 minutes, until smooth, nonsticky, and elastic. Knead in up to 1 more cup of white flour, if necessary. Let the dough rest while you wash, dry, and grease the bowl. Knead the dough another few times, form into a ball, and place it in the bowl. Turn it to coat with oil. Cover with a clean kitchen towel and put in a warm, draft-free place to rise until doubled in bulk, 1 to 1½ hours. It has risen sufficiently when you can gently poke a finger into the dough and the hole remains after a few minutes' wait.

3. Flour your fist and punch down the dough. Knead a few times, then shape into a round, plump loaf and place it on a large, cornmeal-sprinkled baking sheet. Cover with a clean kitchen towel and place it in a warm, draft-free place to double in bulk. Meanwhile, preheat the oven to 375°F.

4. When loaf has doubled, slash it lightly in two places with a sharp knife. Brush it with cold water. Bake it for 1 to 1½ hours, until a knuckle rap produces a hollow sound. Brush with water twice during the baking process. Let cool thoroughly on a rack.

BAGELS

Even though home kitchens lack the ferocious ovens and complex equipment of bagel bakeries, it is still possible to make the real thing at home. In fact, your bagels will be superior to those from many bakeries, considering the proliferation of bagel places across the country producing mediocre bagels that are mere shadows of what they should be.

Bagels have a tough, crunchy exterior and a tender interior. This is achieved by *boiling* the dough before baking it.

Makes 16 to 18

2 packages dried yeast
2 cups warm water (100° to 115°F)
3 tablespoons kosher salt
5½ to 6 cups bread flour
4 tablespoons sugar
1 egg
Kosher salt
Poppy seeds
Sesame seeds

1. Combine the yeast and warm water in a large bowl. Stir with a fork or a small whisk. Add 1 tablespoon salt.

2. Stir in 5 cups of flour, 1 cup at a time.

Use a whisk until the mixture becomes stiff, then switch to a wooden spoon.

3. Use a handful of the remaining flour to flour your work surface. Turn the dough out and knead rhythmically and vigorously, adding more flour as you knead, until the dough is smooth, springy, nonsticky, and elastic. This dough should be quite stiff. It is kneaded sufficiently when you can poke it with your finger and the indentation springs back. Total kneading time will be 10 to 15 minutes.

4. Cover the dough with a cloth and let it rest while you wash, dry, and oil the bowl. Knead the dough a few more turns, then form it into a ball and place in the bowl. Turn to coat with oil. Cover the bowl and put it in a warm, draft-free place until it doubles in bulk (about 1 hour). It has risen sufficiently when you can poke a finger in the dough and the hole remains after about 5 minutes. (Poke very gently or the dough will collapse.)

5. When doubled, flour your fist and punch the dough down. Knead a few times, then allow to rest for a few minutes. Divide the dough into 16 to 18 equal pieces. As you work with one piece, keep the remainder covered with a kitchen towel. Spread another towel out on a clean work surface.

6. Roll each piece of dough between your hands to form a smooth ball. Flatten slightly and use your thumb to form a hole in the center about 1 inch in diameter. Place finished circles on the towel-covered surface.

7. Cover bagels lightly with plastic wrap and let rise for 20 to 30 minutes, until puffy but not quite doubled. In the meantime, preheat the oven to 450°F. Combine 5 quarts water, the sugar, and the remaining 2 tablespoons salt. Bring to a boil. Have one large or two small baking sheets. Cut parchment paper to fit the sheets. Place the paper on sheets and grease lightly.

8. Adjust the water bath to remain at a gentle boil. Four or five at a time, drop the bagels into water. Cook for 3 minutes, turn with tongs, and cook for 2 to 3 minutes on the second side. Remove with a skimmer or slotted spoon, and place briefly back on the towel to drain. Place on a baking sheet.

9. Beat the egg with 1 tablespoon water. Brush the top of each bagel with this mixture, and sprinkle with kosher salt, poppy seeds, or sesame seeds, if desired.

10. Bake in preheated oven for 20 to 30 minutes, until golden brown and crusty. Remove from baking sheets. (You may have to peel off the paper.) Let cool on racks. These freeze beautifully. As soon as they have cooled, seal in plastic bags and freeze. To reheat, place frozen bagels, uncovered, on a baking sheet. Bake in a 350°F oven for 15 minutes.

Note The boiled, unbaked bagels may be frozen at the end of step 8. Let them cool, wrap them well, and freeze until needed. At serving time, place the frozen bagels on a lightly greased parchment-covered baking sheet in a 400°F oven. Bake for 40 to 45 minutes, until brown, crusty, and done. These bagels are even better and crustier than if not frozen.

BAGEL ETIQUETTE

For slicing crusty homemade bread, a long, serrated knife is a good thing to own. Never use that knife, however, on a bagel. Proper bagel behavior demands a fork. With the tines of a fork, perforate the bagel all around its outer perimeter, then separate the bagel into two halves along the dotted line. The texture of the inner surface of each bagel half will be rough and absolutely delicious, whether spread with butter or cheese or served plain. Cut with a knife, the surfaces will be perfectly smooth and the bagel will be insipid. (It may even be flecked with blood if your knife-wielding technique is less than impeccable.)

A very popular way of serving forked bagels is to cover each half with American Münster cheese. Broil until the cheese is runny, gooey, and speckled with brown. Superb snacking!

"The bagel, a form of Jewish baked goods sometimes described as a doughnut with rigor mortis..."
New York Times, February 4, 1956

KAISER ROLLS

These crusty rolls are meant to be slathered with good mustard and piled high with corned beef, pastrami, salami, or tongue. If you wish, sprinkle each roll with poppy seeds before baking. Then, instead of brushing the rolls with water, spray them lightly, using a plant mister or a water pistol. I like to bake small rolls, so everyone can have more than one kind of sandwich. They can be made larger (bake a little longer) if desired.

Makes 12 small rolls or 6 large ones

1 package dried yeast
1 cup warm water (100° to 115°F)
1½ teaspoons kosher salt
3½ to 4 cups bread flour
1 egg
Cornmeal

1. Combine the yeast and warm water in a large bowl. Stir with a fork or a whisk to dissolve yeast.

2. Stir in the salt, 2 cups of flour, and the egg.

3. Add an additional 1½ cups of flour, ½ cup at a time, switching to a wooden spoon as the dough gets stiff.

4. Flour your work surface with a bit of the remaining flour. Turn out the dough and knead rhythmically, adding more of the flour as needed, until the dough is firm, satiny, elastic, and nonsticky. It is kneaded sufficiently when two lightly poked finger depressions spring back. Let the dough rest while you wash, dry, and oil the bowl.

5. Form the dough into a ball. Place it in the bowl and turn to coat it with the oil. Cover and put in a warm, draft-free place to double in bulk (at least 1 hour). When you think it is doubled, gently poke a hole in the risen dough and wait 5 minutes. If the hole remains, the dough is ready.

6. Flour your fist and punch the dough down. Knead a few more times. Divide the dough into 12 even pieces and shape each piece into a round ball. Cover and allow to rise for 20 minutes.

7. Sprinkle a baking sheet with cornmeal.

8. Uncover the dough. Flatten each ball. With the tip of a very sharp small knife, or with a single-edged razor, lightly slash the rolls from the center to the edge, curving as you slash. Make 5 slashes in this manner, evenly spaced. (Keep in mind what a kaiser roll looks like and you'll know exactly how to curve and space the cuts.)

9. Place the rolls on the cornmeal-sprinkled baking sheet. Cover lightly and let rise until doubled in bulk, about 1 hour.

10. Preheat over to 425°F. Place a baking dish on the bottom of the oven and half fill it with boiling water.

11. When the rolls have doubled, brush them with cold water. Bake for 20 minutes, until browned and done. (The larger rolls may take a little longer.) Brush with water three or four times during the baking. Let cool on racks. These freeze well. Thaw by placing, unwrapped, on a baking sheet. Put in a 350°F oven for 15 to 20 minutes.

ONION ROLLS

Serve these tender onion- and poppy-seed-flecked rolls in the bread basket at dinnertime or use them for turkey or roast beef sandwiches. They also make fine hamburger buns.

Makes 15

1 package dried yeast
1 cup warm water (100° to 115°F)
2 tablespoons sugar
2 teaspoons kosher salt
5 to 6 cups unbleached white flour
3 eggs
¼ cup vegetable oil
Onion topping (recipe follows)
1 egg, beaten with 1 tablespoon water, or vegetable oil

1. In a large bowl, combine the yeast and warm water. Stir with a fork or a small whisk.

2. Whisk in the sugar, salt, 2 cups flour, eggs, and oil.

3. Stir in 3 more cups of flour, 1 cup at a time. As the dough gets stiff, switch from the whisk to a wooden spoon.

4. Flour your work surface with some of the remaining flour. Turn out the dough and knead rhythmically, adding a bit more flour as needed, until the dough is smooth, non-sticky, satiny, and elastic. This will take about 10 minutes in all. Let the dough rest, covered, while you wash, dry, and oil the bowl.

5. Form the dough into a ball. Place it in the bowl, and turn it so that it is coated with oil. Cover the bowl and place it in a warm, draft-free place to double in bulk, about 1 hour. To check if it has risen sufficiently, gently poke a finger hole in the dough and wait 5 minutes. If the hole does not close up, the dough is ready.

6. Flour your fist and punch the dough down. Knead a few times. Pull off 15 equal pieces of dough, rolling each into a tight round, smooth ball before you pull off another. As they are formed into balls, place them under a towel.

7. Grease one large or two small baking sheets. Have the onion topping ready.

8. One at a time, flatten each ball of dough slightly. Place on the baking sheet.

9. Brush each roll with the egg wash if you want the crust to be glazed or with vegetable oil if you want it soft. Sprinkle on the topping. (Keep some rolls plain, if desired.) Cover lightly and put in a warm, draft-free place to double in bulk, about ½ hour.

10. Preheat the oven to 400°F.

11. When doubled, bake for 15 minutes, or until browned and cooked through. These rolls freeze well. To thaw, wrap the frozen rolls in foil and place in a 350°F oven for 15 to 20 minutes.

Onion Topping
½ cup finely minced onion
½ teaspoon kosher salt
½ tablespoon poppy seeds
½ cup dry bread crumbs
2 tablespoons vegetable oil

Mix well in a small bowl.

Sandwiches

"The Reuben, of course, was named for New York's famous delicatessen deluxe... you can find the Reuben all over the country... and it varies in quality from excellent to awful."

JAMES BEARD
Beard on Food, 1974

HOME-CURED CORNED BEEF

I did a lot of research and cured many briskets trying to find the safest, easiest, and most delicious homemade corned beef. This method uses a commercial curing salt, available in the salt and spice departments of many supermarkets (otherwise, see the Source Guide, page 94). Follow the directions exactly when weighing the meat and measuring the salt. The rest of the seasonings may be adjusted to taste, although I think this balance is just about perfect. I like the faintest hint of cloves in my corned beef. Some people do not, so leave it out if you wish. The technique of dry-curing in a bag takes up a minimum amount of space in the refrigerator, and the foil-wrapped roasting is utterly simple. The finished corned beef will be extremely juicy, mild, and unsalty, with a complex play of seasonings that fill the mouth yet are not overpowering or vulgar.

6 large garlic cloves, peeled
3 Turkish bay leaves
⅛ scant teaspoon whole cloves (optional)
2 heaping tablespoons whole coriander seeds
2 heaping tablespoons whole black peppercorns
1 heaping tablespoon whole mustard seeds
¼ cup dark brown sugar, well packed
1 first-cut beef brisket, trimmed of all but a very thin layer of top fat (about 4 pounds)
Morton's Tender Quick Curing Salt

1. Put the garlic, bay leaves, cloves, coriander seeds, peppercorns, and mustard seeds in the container of an electric blender. Blend until coarsely ground. Scrape into a bowl. Toss in the brown sugar.

2. Weigh the trimmed brisket. Carefully measure out 1 level tablespoon of curing salt per pound of meat. (If the meat weighs 3 ½ pounds, measure out 3 ½ tablespoons of salt). Add the salt to the other seasonings.

3. Rub the seasoning mixture into all sides of the meat. Press it in well. Put the meat in a sturdy plastic food storage bag. Tie securely, place in a shallow pan, and refrigerate. Leave in the refrigerator to cure for 5 days per inch thickness of meat (measure at the thickest point). Turn the bag once a day.

4. At the end of the curing period, remove the meat from the bag. Pour out the accumulated juices. Do not scrape off the embedded spices. Preheat the oven to 300°F.

5. Tear off a large sheet of heavy-duty aluminum foil, large enough to enclose the corned beef. Wrap the corned beef well, crimping the edges of the foil tightly so that no juices or steam can escape. Put in the oven for 2 to 3 hours, until the meat is tender when pierced with a skewer. Slice and serve, or wrap and refrigerate. To reheat, slice and steam the slices over boiling water for 3 to 5 minutes.

STORE-BOUGHT CORNED BEEF

Many different brands of Cryovac-sealed corned beef are available in supermarket meat sections across the country. They range in quality from decent to dreadful. You will have to experiment until you find a brand you like. Some companies offer corned beef rounds as well as corned beef briskets. Always choose a brisket; it is a much juicier cut of meat. After cooking, you may find that the meat seems pulpy or stringy. The chilling period firms it up again. On the next day, the meat will have a good texture and will slice beautifully.

Serves 6

1 corned beef brisket (3 to 4 pounds)
1 potato with skin
1 celery stalk with leaves
1 onion with skin
2 carrots, unpeeled

1. Remove the corned beef from its wrapping. Rinse well under cold running water. Put it in a large pot with the vegetables. Pour in cold water to cover 4 inches above the meat. Cover the pot and bring to a boil. Reduce the heat and simmer, covered, for 25 minutes.

2. Drain the meat and vegetables in a colander. Return them to the pot. Pour in fresh cold water to cover 4 inches above the meat. Cover the pot and bring to a boil.

3. Reduce the heat and simmer very slowly, covered, for 3 hours or more, until the meat is very tender when tested with a skewer. Drain well. Wrap with plastic wrap and refrigerate for at least 12 hours.

TO SLICE AND REHEAT COOKED CORNED BEEF

1. Cut the chilled corned beef into thin slices against the grain.

2. Place a steamer over boiling water. Put the corned beef slices in the steamer, cover, and steam for 5 minutes. Remove with tongs.

REUBEN

This has become a classic in non-kosher delis. I prefer the sandwich with a thin layer of meat, although it is traditional in many delis to pile it to the sky.

Rye bread (page 59)
Russian dressing (page 15)
Thinly sliced corned beef (pages 66–67)
Well-drained fresh sauerkraut (page 46)
Sliced Swiss cheese
Butter

1. Spread slices of rye bread with Russian dressing, pile on some corned beef, pile some sauerkraut over the beef, and top with a slice of Swiss cheese. Cover with another slice of Russian-dressing-spread rye.

2. Butter the outside of the top and bottom slices of bread and toast in a toaster oven, or in a large heavy skillet. When the bread is nicely toasted, the filling is hot, and the cheese is melted, serve at once.

TURKEY REUBEN Substitute sliced turkey and health salad (page 76) for the corned beef and sauerkraut.

DELI HOT DOGS

First you have to find the real thing—frankfurters made with sheep-intestine casings—no easy feat these days. (It doesn't pay to try this with any other hot dog.) Then you have to boil with care. The idea is to boil the sausage so that its juices swell up and *almost* burst out of the skin. Just at the exquisite point of almost-but-not-quite-bursting (the skin must *never* split) the hot dog must be quickly plucked from its bath, frantically blotted dry, thrust into a bun, smeared, festooned, and devoured. At the first bite, the teeth shatter the tough casing and the hot juicy sausage flesh explodes in the mouth. I shudder with anticipation every time I plunge a frankfurter into the wildly boiling pot of water. If you have no meat or sausage company in your vicinity supplying the proper sausages, you might consider moving.

Frankfurters or knackwurst in natural
    casings
Hot dog buns
Deli mustard (page 14)
Sauerkraut (page 46)

1. Bring enough water to a boil to cover the hot dogs by 2 inches.

2. Put the sausages in the boiling water. Al-low frankfurters to boil hard for 10 minutes, knackwurst for 15 minutes. (Timing varies with the size of the hot dogs, so watch carefully.)

3. Remove the sausages from water with tongs. Blot dry quickly on paper towels and insert in the buns. Smear with mustard, top with a drippy heap of sauerkraut, and eat at once.

PASTRAMI

If you own or have access to a smoker, you can (oh joy!) make pastrami at home. Chuck deckle (try a kosher butcher) is best. But if it is hard to find, brisket makes a very decent pastrami too. My pastrami advisor, Leo Steiner of the Carnegie Deli, says that a brisket produces "Canadian smoked spiced beef, not *real* pastrami". It may not be *real,* but it's awfully good.

Chuck deckle or brisket (3 to 4 pounds)
4 large garlic cloves
2 heaping tablespoons coriander seeds
4 heaping tablespoons whole black
    peppercorns
1 tablespoon ground ginger
¼ cup dark brown sugar, well packed
Morton's Tender Quick Curing Salt

1. Cure the meat following the directions for home cured corned beef (see page 66) using the above spice mixture.

2. When the meat is cured, remove it from the bag and pour out the accumulated liquid. Do not scrape off the spices. Use a trussing needle and kitchen string to make a hanging loop through the narrow end of the meat.

3. Hang the meat in a cool (70°F or less) spot in front of an electric fan. Leave to dry for 24 hours.

4. Following manufacturer's directions for your smoker, smoke at 150°F for 2 hours.

5. Preheat the oven to 300°F. Remove hanging string from the smoked meat. Wrap the meat in heavy duty foil so that no steam or juices can escape. Cook in the oven for 2 to 3 hours or until very tender. Slice against the grain and serve hot.

Note To reheat, place slices in a steamer and steam for 3 to 5 minutes.

ROASTED BRISKET

Hot or cold brisket, with gravy and deli mustard, on rye or a hard roll, makes a magnificent sandwich. It bears an astounding taste resemblance to the classic "debris" po' boy of New Orleans.

Serves 6

1 (4-pound) first-cut brisket of beef, trimmed of all but a thin layer of fat on top
3 tablespoons vegetable oil
6 large onions, coarsely chopped
6 large garlic cloves, peeled and lightly crushed
½ cup dry white wine
Salt and freshly ground pepper to taste

1. Preheat the oven to 350°F.

2. Dry the brisket with paper towels and, starting with the fat side first, brown well on both sides. (The meat will render enough of its own fat for browning.) Place on a platter and cover lightly.

3. Drain the drippings from the skillet. Heat the oil in the skillet. Toss the onions into the oil. Cover the skillet and steam over low heat for 10 minutes. Uncover, raise the heat, and cook the onions until they are deeply browned. Toss in the garlic.

4. Pour in the wine. Bring to a boil, stirring and scraping the bottom of the skillet with a wooden spoon to dislodge the browned bits. Boil until the wine is completely gone. Season with salt and pepper.

5. Spread the onions on the bottom of a shallow baking dish. Season the brisket with salt and pepper. Place it, fat side up, on the onions. Pour in any meat juices that have accumulated on the platter. Seal the dish very well with heavy-duty foil and place in the oven for ½ hour.

6. Turn oven down to 250°F and bake for an additional 2½ hours, or until the meat is very tender. At the end of each hour, with a large cooking spoon spoon out the rendered liquid into a glass jar, leaving the onions in the pan. Re-cover tightly with foil and return to the oven. Cover the jar and refrigerate.

7. When the brisket is tender, remove from the oven. Pour in the reserved meat liquid. Cover tightly and refrigerate. On the next day, scrape off the hardened fat and discard. Remove the meat to a cutting board. Pour the meat juices into a saucepan and boil until reduced slightly. Meanwhile, slice the brisket against the grain. Return to the baking pan with the reduced meat broth and onions. Serve hot or cold, or store in the refrigerator for a day or so until needed.

"Mustard's no good without roast beef."
CHICO MARX
in the movie *Monkey Business*, 1931

DELI ROAST BEEF

Retired kosher butcher Bernie Russo revealed the secret of old-time deli roast beef when he told me about this cut of beef. When roasted to the rare stage, it is remarkably tender and flavorful—perfect for deli sandwiches. The technique of allowing the onions and liquid in the pan to cook down produces a dark, rich gravy. Use the gravy cold, as a spread for the roast beef sandwiches.

Makes about 2 pounds sliced beef

1 eye of chuck roast (approximately 2 ½ pounds)
Freshly ground pepper and salt to taste
1 large onion, cut in half and sliced into half-moons
Beef or chicken broth
Dry white or red wine

1. Preheat the oven 350°F.

2. Place the roast on a rack in a 10-inch-square glass-ceramic baking dish that will work on top of the stove as well as in the oven. While the roast is in the dish, sprinkle it on all sides with a generous amount of freshly ground pepper and a modest amount of salt.

3. Put onion slices in the dish. Pour in approximately ¼ cup each of broth and wine. Put in the oven.

4. When just about all the liquid has evaporated and a burned encrustation has formed on the bottom of the pan, pour in another ¼ cup each broth and wine. Roast the meat for only 45 to 55 minutes in all, until an instant-read thermometer inserted in the thickest part of the roast reads 120°F. During the roasting time add more broth and wine occasionally, but there is no need to baste the roast.

5. Remove the roast to a platter. Let it rest at room temperature for at least 20 minutes. Remove the rack from the roasting dish and place the dish on the stove. Bring the pan juices with their onions to a boil, stirring and scraping up the burned encrustations in the dish. When the juices are dark brown, thick, and syrupy, remove from heat. Stir in meat juices that have accumulated under the roast. Pour into a small jar, cover and refrigerate.

6. Trim the roast of covering fat. Wrap the roast in plastic wrap, then in foil, and refrigerate until needed.

7. To slice the meat, use a very sharp carving knife. Slice on the diagonal into thin, wide slices. The slices from the front of the roast will have a bit of connective tissue running through the top. You can cut these slices in half and discard the tough tissue. Serve on hard rolls (page 62) with deli mustard (page 14) spread on one half and some of the cold pan juices with their onions on the other.

PICKLED TONGUE

Tongue is pickled by the same method as brisket (page 66). The finished tongue will be very tender and delicious. The slices, even when cold, are unbelievably supple and succulent. Because the tongue is covered with a tough skin, prick it all over with a sharp skewer before rubbing in the spice-curing salt mixture. Use the same spice mixture, weigh the tongue and measure out the curing salt in exactly the same way as in the home-cured corned beef recipe (page 66). Measure the tongue's thickness and cure for five days per inch, turning the bag once a day.

1. Once pickled, remove the tongue from the plastic bag and pour out the accumulated juices. Do not scrape off the spices. Preheat the oven to 300°F.

2. Wrap the tongue in heavy duty aluminum foil so that no steam or juices can escape. Cook in the oven for 2½ to 3½ hours. It is done when the two little bones at the thick end pull out easily.

3. Trim the thick end. Slit the skin, peel it off, and slice the tongue thinly. Peel only as much as you wish to use. Store the remainder, unpeeled and well-wrapped, in the refrigerator.

TONGUE'S FOR THE MEMORY

In delis, sandwiches are *very large,* and in some the monsters have names. Here are a few examples from the menu of the Carnegie Deli in New York City. The list should give you plenty of ideas for building deli sandwiches in your own kitchen. Remember, to be authentically deli, a sandwich must be overstuffed. At the Carnegie, a single corned beef sandwich holds ¾ pound of meat. The bread must be a good, fresh, crunchy crusted rye, pumpernickel, or hard roll. You cannot make a deli sandwich on packaged bread.

Tongue's for the Memory: Tongue, Corned Beef, Swiss Cheese, Coleslaw, and Russian Dressing

Carnegie Haul: Pastrami, Tongue, and Salami

Nova on Sunday: Nova Scotia Smoked Salmon, Lake Sturgeon, Bermuda Onion, Lettuce, Tomato, Olives, and Cream Cheese

Nosh, Nosh Nanette: Open-Faced Hot Turkey with Gravy

Beef Encounter: Roast Beef, Chopped Liver, and Bermuda Onion

Leo's Delightin: Turkey, Corned Beef, Tongue, Coleslaw, and Russian Dressing

The Egg and Oy: Chicken Salad, Sliced Egg, Lettuce and Tomato

50 Ways to Love Your Liver: Chopped Liver, Hard-Boiled Egg, and Onion

Brisketball: Brisket of Beef, White-Meat Turkey, Onion, Lettuce and Tomato

Salads

"Elka had laid out her famous tiny meat knishes, the matzoh meal pancakes, the deli trays of corned beef, pastrami, chopped liver, and potato salad; the lox and cream cheese, cold kippers...and smoked whitefish; stacks of corn rye and a nice pumpernickel; cole slaw, chicken salad; and flotillas of cucumber pickles."

HARLAN ELLISON
Strange Wine, 1979

QUALITY'S POTATO SALAD

Fay Robinson and Georgia Richardson at Atlanta's tiny Quality Kosher Deli turn out the *best* potato salad in the world. The salad is unusual because it is made with Idahos. When the potatoes are chopped, they mash up a bit. When mixed with mayonnaise, they mash even more. The final texture is compellingly smooth and creamy.

Serves 6

3 pounds Idaho potatoes, scrubbed
1 small carrot, peeled
½ celery stalk
½ small green pepper
½ small onion
1 tablespoon sugar
Salt to taste
¾ cup mayonnaise
Grated carrot for garnish
Chopped green pepper for garnish

WHAT TO DRINK WITH A DELI MEAL?

Hot tea in a glass is good. So is beer. Celery tonic and cream soda are even better. But seltzer, that sparkling, ineffably refreshing draft, is best. And the only after-dinner potable to even consider is an egg cream.

1. Boil potatoes in a generous amount of salted water until thoroughly tender.

2. While they are cooking, shred the carrot, celery, and pepper, using the shredding disk of a food processor or the large holes on a four-sided grater. Grate the onion on the grater. There should be about 1 cup of vegetables in all.

3. When the potatoes are tender, drain in a colander. Run cold water over them until they are cool enough to handle, but do not cool thoroughly. For best results, the potatoes must be warm when the mayonnaise is added. With a table knife, scrape off the skins.

4. Place the potatoes in a large wooden bowl or on a wooden chopping surface. With a hand chopper (see page 9), chop the potatoes. As you chop, the potatoes will mash slightly.

5. Put the potatoes in a large bowl. Squeeze any liquid out of the shredded vegetables. Add the vegetables to the potatoes. Sprinkle with sugar and salt. Mix lightly.

6. With a wooden spoon, fold in the mayonnaise. As you fold, the potatoes will mash even more. When everything is well combined, refrigerate until serving time.

7. For the true deli look, put the potato salad in a serving dish and cover one half of its surface with grated carrot, the other with chopped green pepper.

POTATO SALAD

This potato salad contains no mayonnaise. The oil and vinegar dressing must be added while the potatoes are still warm, so that it will be fully absorbed.

Serves 6

3 pounds small, new potatoes
½ cup olive oil
3 tablespoons white wine vinegar
½ cup fresh chopped parsley
½ cup thinly sliced scallions
Salt and freshly ground pepper to taste

1. Boil the potatoes in a generous amount of salted water until cooked but not at all mushy. Drain well.

2. Cut the potatoes while still warm into ¼-inch-thick slices and place in a bowl.

3. Add the oil and vinegar and toss very gently. Add the parsley, scallions, and salt and pepper and toss gently again. Serve warm or at room temperature.

COLESLAW

Serves 6 to 8

2 pounds cabbage, cored and trimmed of
    tough veiny outer leaves
1 cup grated carrots
½ cup grated white radish
½ cup sliced scallions
½ cup fresh chopped parsley
½ cup pitted, sliced black Greek olives
    (optional)
8 tablespoons vegetable oil
3 tablespoons wine vinegar
4 tablespoons mayonnaise
3 tablespoons lemon juice
Salt and freshly ground pepper to taste

1. Slice the cabbage into thin shreds using the slicing disk of a food processor or a chef's knife. There will be about 6 cups of cabbage in all. Use the processor's grating disk when grating the other vegetables, or use the large holes on a four-sided grater. Combine all vegetables and the olives in a bowl.

2. Combine the remaining ingredients in a screw-top jar. Cover and shake until very well combined.

3. Pour the dressing over the vegetables and toss gently to combine. Serve at once.

HEALTH SALAD

At the 2nd Avenue Deli, this sweet-and-sour coleslaw sits in a bowl on every table right next to the pickles.

Serves 6 to 8

2 pounds cabbage, cored and trimmed of
    tough veiny outer leaves
1 large red pepper, cored and seeded
2 large carrots, peeled
2 celery stalks
3 tablespoons oil
3 tablespoons sugar
5 tablespoons white vinegar
Salt and freshly ground pepper to taste

1. If you have a food processor, the vegetables are easily prepared. Slice the cabbage and the red pepper into thin shreds with the slicing disk. Grate the carrots and celery on the shredding disk. Lacking a food processor, use a sharp knife for the cabbage and pepper and the large holes on a four-sided grater for the carrots and celery. There will be about 6 cups of cabbage in all.

2. Combine the vegetables in a large bowl. Add the oil and toss to coat the vegetables. In a screwtop jar, combine the sugar, vinegar, and salt and pepper. Cover the jar and shake until the sugar is dissolved. Toss this mixture into the cabbage.

3. Refrigerate the salad for an hour. Taste and adjust the seasonings before serving. The salad may be refrigerated overnight if there are leftovers. On the next day it will be wilted, but still absolutely delicious.

SIDNEY'S EGG SALAD

Sidney Glazer used to hold a wonderful New York-deli-style brunch every Sunday at his Atlanta restaurant, Sidney's Just South. Sidney and chef Patrick Burke developed this egg salad for the brunch. The fresh ginger added to the traditional egg-mayonnaise mix is a touch of genius.

Makes 4 cups

12 eggs, at room temperature
1½ cups mayonnaise
1 heaping teaspoon grated ginger
Salt and freshly ground pepper to taste
2 tablespoons chopped fresh parsley
1 small onion, minced
½ cup Greek black olives, pitted and
    coarsely chopped

1. Put the eggs in a nonreactive saucepan and pour in cold water to cover by 1 inch. Bring to a boil. Immediately turn off the heat and clap the cover on the pan. Let stand for 10 minutes.

2. Drain and immediately run very cold water over eggs until they are completely cooled (about 5 minutes).

3. Peel and chop the eggs. Add the remaining ingredients except the olives and mix well.

4. Scrape the salad into a serving bowl. Garnish around the perimeter with the olives. Chill for several hours, for flavors to develop.

WHITEFISH SALAD

A scoop of whitefish salad is the basis for the best deli salad platter of all. The smokiness of the fish gives the salad a very seductive flavor.

Makes 2 cups

4 ounces sable (smoked cod)
3 (4-ounce) smoked whitefish
½ cup mayonnaise
Juice of ½ lemon
Freshly ground pepper
2 tablespoons chopped chives
2 tablespoons parsley
¼ to ½ cup sour cream

1. Discard the skin from the sable and the skin, bones, head, and tail from the whitefish. Make sure that no little bones are left on the fish. Flake the meat from both fish. Put in a bowl.

2. Gently fold in the remaining ingredients except the sour cream. Chill for several hours or overnight.

3. Just before serving, fold in the sour cream. Taste, adjust the seasonings, and serve.

CHICKEN SALAD

Boiling a chicken *hard* for a short time produces a moist, succulent bird without a trace of pulpiness. I learned this Oriental trick from a Chinese friend when he taught me to make bon bon chicken. This salad may be made in advance, but do not add the scallions until a few hours before serving. Don't leave the chicken to cool beyond the specified time, and be sure to refrigerate it in a shallow dish. Both factors are important in preventing bacterial growth that could cause food poisoning.

Makes 4 cups

1 chicken (3½ pounds)
½ cup mayonnaise
Juice of ½ large lemon, or more to taste
Salt and freshly ground pepper to taste
¼ cup chopped fresh parsley
¼ cup thinly sliced scallions (green and
    white parts)
1 celery stalk, cut in half lengthwise and
    sliced

1. Bring 6 quarts of water to a boil in a deep pot.

2. Pull excess fat from chicken and wash the bird well, inside and out, in cold water. Submerge the chicken in the boiling water. When the water returns to a full rolling boil, clap on the cover and boil hard for 18 minutes.

3. Remove from the heat and allow the chicken to cool in the covered pot for 2 hours.

4. Remove it from the cooking liquid. (It will still be quite warm, so handle with care.) Remove the skin. Pull all the chicken meat off the bone in large pieces. Discard all tendons and gristle. Tear the meat into 2-inch chunks. Put in a bowl.

5. Gently combine the chicken with the mayonnaise. Fold in the remaining ingredients. Taste and add additional lemon juice, salt, and pepper as needed. The salad may be served at once, or chilled. Store in the refrigerator, spread out in a shallow dish, and well covered with plastic wrap.

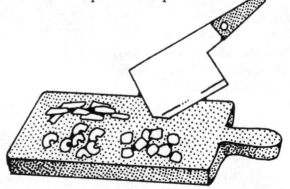

Brunch

"Protect your bagels—put lox on them!"
Sign, Goldberg and Son's
Bagel Bakery and Deli
Atlanta, 1984

HOME-CURED LOX

Lox is raw salmon that has been salt-cured. You can easily make lox at home, less salty and more delicious than that available from many delis. Imagine the heady sense of pride at serving a brunch where the bagels, the lox, and the cream cheese are all homemade. The salmon, once cured, will keep in the refrigerator for approximately 5 days.

Serves 6 to 8

¼ cup kosher salt
¼ cup sugar
1 to 2 tablespoons freshly ground pepper
1 ½ pounds center-cut salmon fillet in one
  piece, with skin

1. Combine the salt, sugar, and pepper. Spread half of the mixture on the bottom of a shallow glass baking dish of a size to hold the salmon comfortably.

2. With tweezers, remove any small bones left in the salmon. Dry the salmon well with paper towels. Rub the skin side with a little bit of the remaining salt-sugar mixture. Rub the rest of the mixture into the other side of the fish. Place the fish, skin side down, in the glass dish. Cover well with plastic wrap.

3. Place another dish on top of the salmon. Cover with a cutting board and place a weight on the board—a clean brick or some heavy canned goods. Refrigerate for 72 hours. Every 12 hours, remove the weights, unwrap the fish, and baste with the liquid that has accumulated in the dish. Then re-wrap, re-cover, and return to the refrigerator.

4. At the end of the 3-day period, remove the fish from the dish and scrape off the remaining pepper. Dry, wrap well in plastic wrap, and return to refrigerator for one more day.

5. To serve, place skin side down on a cutting board. With a thin, sharp carving knife, slice thinly on the diagonal, detaching the flesh from the skin as you slice. Serve with bagels (page 60), cream cheese (page 81), tomatoes, and sliced sweet onion.

YOGURT CREAM CHEESE

Drain yogurt for 24 hours and you will have a creamy, tangy cheese, perfect for spreading on toasted bagels. The cheese is particularly good mixed with fresh chives.

Makes about 10 ounces

2 quarts yogurt
Salt (optional)
Flavoring of your choice: chopped fresh dill or chives, crushed garlic marinated in wine vinegar, or shredded smoked whitefish or lox

1. Line a sieve or colander with a long piece of doubled damp cheesecloth and place it over a large bowl. Dump in the yogurt, fold the cheesecloth over to cover well, and leave in a cool part of your kitchen for 24 hours. Every once in a while, pour off the liquid that accumulates in the bowl.

2. At the end of the 24-hour period, pick up the wrapped ball of yogurt cheese and squeeze it over the bowl to extract any remaining liquid. Place the cheese in a bowl and mix in salt to taste (although it is perfectly delicious with no salt at all) and—if you wish—the flavoring of your choice. Refrigerate for several hours before serving. If the yogurt is fresh to begin with, the cream cheese will keep for weeks.

SUNDAY BRUNCH

One of the best of all deli meals is Sunday brunch. Offer overflowing baskets of bagels, along with butter, plain and flavored cream cheeses, thick slices of tomato and sweet onion, black Greek olives, potato salad, health salad, and an array of all the beautiful varieties of smoked and cured fish that you can carry home from the nearest deli.

A good deli or appetizing store will have a staggering array. Look for:
• Hand-sliced Nova Scotia smoked salmon This is smoked with charcoal and hickory chips. (If the fish is actually from Nova Scotia, it is called "Nova Scotia salmon." If it is Pacific salmon, it should be called simply "Nova.")
• Lox (salt-cured raw salmon)
• Kippered salmon (hot-smoke-cooked in ovens that are equipped with charcoal for a smoky flavor)
• Whole smoked whitefish
• Sable (smoked cod that has been spiced with hot paprika)
• Smoked sturgeon
• Pickled herring fillets

SMOKED SALMON PIZZA, SPAGO

Wolfgang Puck, the young culinary wizard of Spago in Los Angeles, has put together some traditional deli ingredients and come up with a very upscale version of bagels and lox. This recipe originally appeared in *Food and Wine* magazine.

Serves 4

3 cups unbleached flour, or as needed
1 envelope yeast
1 teaspoon salt
1 tablespoon clover honey
6 tablespoons olive oil
2 teaspoons minced chives
6 tablespoons sour cream
8 large thin slices of smoked salmon or homemade lox (about 4 ounces)
2 ounces golden caviar (whitefish roe)

1. In a food processor, briefly mix the flour and the yeast.

2. In a small bowl, mix the salt, honey, 2 tablespoons olive oil, and ¾ cup of water. With the motor running, slowly pour the liquid into the processor. Process until the dough masses together on the blade, using up to an additional ¼ cup water if necessary. (The yeast will not be fully incorporated at this point; it will be incorporated only after rising.)

3. Transfer the dough to a lightly floured surface. Knead 1 teaspoon chives into the dough. Continue kneading, adding more flour if necessary to prevent sticking, until smooth and satiny, about 5 minutes. Put the dough in a lightly oiled bowl, turn once to oil the surface, then cover with a damp kitchen towel and let rise until doubled in size, about 30 minutes.

4. Turn the dough out onto a lightly floured surface. Cut into quarters and roll each quarter into a tight smooth ball. Place them on a baking sheet, cover with a damp kitchen towel, and refrigerate until baking time. They may remain refrigerated for 3 hours.

5. One hour before baking time, remove the dough from the refrigerator and let it return to room temperature. Preheat the oven to 500° F.

6. On a lightly floured surface, flatten one of the balls of dough into a 6-inch circle, leaving the outer edge thicker than the center. Gently stretch the edge to form an 8-inch circle. Crimp the edge to form a small lip. Place the circle of dough on a heavy baking sheet and brush with 1 tablespoon of olive oil. Repeat with the remaining dough and oil.

7. Bake the dough in the bottom third of the oven for about 10 minutes, until golden brown.

8. Spread each hot crust with 1 ½ tablespoons sour cream and top with 2 slices of the smoked salmon. Place a spoonful of the caviar in the center of each pizza. Sprinkle with the remaining chives and serve warm.

"In the Alaskan tundra or on the banks of the Ganges, New Yorkers yearn for the delis of Manhattan."

CRAIG CLAIBORNE
New York Times, August 1974

CHALLAH FRENCH TOAST

Challah makes wonderful French toast, and delis always feature it on their brunch menus. This very special recipe turns French toast into something approaching a soufflé. It is the kind of dish that can make your reputation as a cook. Be sure everyone is seated in time for your mad rush from oven to table. Like a soufflé, the French toast will deflate if made to wait.

Serves 6

6 ounces stale challah
1 teaspoon softened butter
¼ pound melted butter
4 eggs
½ cup sugar
2 cups half-and-half
1 teaspoon cinnamon or 1 teaspoon
    vanilla extract
Maple syrup (optional)

1. Cut the challah into 6 slices.

2. Choose a shallow baking dish that can hold the slices without overlapping and grease it with the softened butter. Place the challah in the dish. Pour the melted butter evenly over the bread.

3. Beat the eggs with the sugar. Beat in the half-and-half and cinnamon. Pour over the bread. Let it soak for several hours at room temperature or overnight in the refrigerator. With a pancake turner, turn the slices once in a while. Be very careful—the bread should not break up. Once the bread is thoroughly saturated with the egg mixture, leave it alone.

4. If it has remained in the refrigerator overnight, bring to room temperature before baking. Preheat the oven to 350°F. Bake, uncovered, for 45 minutes, until puffed and golden. Rush it to the table *at once*. Pass the syrup.

CHEESE BLINTZES

A blintze is a crêpe. The best blintzes are filled with cheese and lightly fried. In these blintzes, the vanilla-and-orange-scented filling is creamy, the outer wrapper delicately crisp. The play of one against the other is ravishing.

Makes 16 to 18

1 cup unbleached flour
Pinch of salt
2 eggs
2 egg yolks
2 tablespoons butter, melted and cooled
    slightly
3 tablespoons orange liqueur (optional)
¾ cup milk
½ cup melted butter
Cheese filling (recipe follows)
Clarified butter
Sour cream

1. Put the flour, salt, eggs, and yolks in the container of a blender. Blend until smooth and well combined. Scrape down the sides of the container.

2. Add the butter, liqueur, milk, and ½ cup water. Blend well. Let the batter stand for at least an hour.

3. Use a heavy, nonstick 6-inch omelet or crêpe pan. Have melted butter and a pastry brush on hand, and a bowl containing the batter. Cover your work surface with wax paper.

4. Heat the pan. Brush with melted butter. With a ladle or scoop that holds about ¼ cup, ladle batter into the hot pan. Immediately tilt the pan so the batter covers the bottom and sides. Pour any excess batter back into the batter bowl.

5. When the batter begins to bubble a bit and come away from the sides of the pan (in just a few seconds), turn the crêpe onto the wax paper, cooked side up. Repeat until the batter is used up.

6. Spread 1 heaping tablespoon of cheese filling along one side of each crêpe. Fold in the opposite sides of each crêpe and then roll up like a jelly roll into a neat package.

7. Place them, seam side down, in one layer on a platter. Cover with plastic wrap and refrigerate until serving time.

8. To serve, melt clarified butter in a deep heavy frying pan to a depth of ¼ inch. Gently fry the blintzes on both sides until golden brown. Serve at once with sour cream.

9. Alternatively, the blintzes may be baked in a 425°F oven until browned.

Cheese Filling

1 pound farmer cheese
4 ounces cream cheese
1 egg
1 egg yolk
Pinch of salt
4 tablespoons sugar
1 teaspoon vanilla extract
Grated rind of 1 orange

Combine all the ingredients in the container of a food processor. Process until smooth and creamy.

MATZOH BREI, QUALITY KOSHER DELI

Fay Robinson at Quality Kosher could win prizes for her fried matzoh, a traditional Passover dish that can be served year-round. This is her version of the all-time classic deli breakfast dish.

Serves 1

2 matzohs
2 eggs
Salt and pepper to taste
2 tablespoons butter

1. Break the matzohs up into large pieces. Soak in cold water for a few seconds. Drain.

2. Beat the eggs with salt and pepper.

3. Melt the butter in a 6-inch skillet or omelet pan. Add the matzoh to the butter. Fry for a minute or so, turning it in the butter.

4. Add the eggs. Stir and fry over moderate heat until dry, crisp and a bit brown. Serve at once.

VARIATIONS Substitute a pinch of sugar for the salt and pepper and serve the matzoh brei with jam or preserves.

Add browned onions (page 12) to the eggs in step 4.

ONION AND EGGS

There are people who could happily eat this for breakfast every day of their lives. Serve it with toasted bagels.

Serves 1

2 tablespoons butter
1 large onion, cut in half and sliced
    into half-moons
3 eggs
Salt and freshly ground pepper to taste

1. Heat the butter in a heavy skillet. Toss the onion into the skillet. Cover and steam over low heat for 10 minutes.

2. Uncover and raise the heat. Sauté, stirring occasionally until the onion is amber and speckled with dark brown, but still retains a hint of crispness.

3. Scrape the onion and its butter into a 10-inch nonstick omelet pan. Heat.

4. Beat the eggs with salt and pepper. Pour into the omelet pan. Over low heat, stir the onion and eggs until creamy and set. Serve at once.

ONION AND EGGS WITH CHEESE Stir in some diced American Münster cheese when the eggs are just barely set. Stir for a few seconds until the cheese melts in streaks throughout the eggs. Serve at once.

LOX AND ONION AND EGGS Stir in 2 ounces of shredded Nova, just before adding the eggs. Omit the salt.

Desserts

"Legendary New York Cheesecake: The richest dessert in history; pure edible ivory, like some new element on the atomic chart—perhaps a fusion of lead and satin."

JANE AND MICHAEL STERN
Goodfood, 1983

NEW YORK CHEESECAKE

Monte Weiner, the man in charge of dessert at Carnegie Deli, believes that cheesecake should have a crumb crust, because a pastry crust would interfere with one's appreciation of the cheesecake's remarkable creamy richness. I agree. A perfect cheesecake should have a crumb crust and *no* fruit topping.

Makes 1 ten-inch cheesecake

Crust

1½ cups graham cracker crumbs
¼ cup sugar
6 tablespoons melted butter

Filling

5 (8-ounce) packages cream cheese, at room temperature
3 tablespoons unbleached flour
1¾ cups sugar
3 tablespoons vanilla extract
3 tablespoons fresh lemon juice
5 whole eggs
2 egg yolks
¼ cup heavy cream

1. Combine the crumbs and sugar. Add the melted butter and mix to moisten. Press this mixture on the bottom and partway up the sides of a 10-inch springform pan. Place in the refrigerator to chill while making filling.

2. Preheat the oven to 500°F.

3. Cream the cream cheese in an electric mixer with a paddle attachment until soft and fluffy.

4. With the paddle, beat in the flour. Beat in the sugar, a little bit at a time. Beat in the vanilla extract, lemon juice, eggs and egg yolks, one at a time, and cream, beating very well between each addition.

5. Pour the cheese mixture into the springform pan. Bake at 500°F for 12 minutes.

6. Turn the oven down to 200°F and bake for 45 minutes.

7. Turn the oven off and leave the cake in the oven for 15 minutes.

8. Remove the pan from the oven and let cool on a rack for 1 hour.

9. Refrigerate the cake in the pan for 5 hours before removing side of pan. This is very important; the cake may collapse if the 5-hour period is cut short.

RUGELACH

These classic cookies—nut-filled crescents—are very popular in Jewish delis and bakeries. The cream cheese dough is versatile. In addition to rugelach, use it for piecrust, sweet and savory turnovers, or even strudel.

Makes 32

8 ounces cream cheese
8 ounces butter
2 cups unbleached flour
Confectioners' sugar
½ cup granulated sugar
½ cup raisins
½ teaspoon cinnamon
1 cup chopped walnuts

1. Remove the cream cheese and butter from refrigerator and let soften for ½ hour.

2. Put the cream cheese, butter, and flour in a bowl and work it all together with your hands until smoothly amalgamated. Form into a ball, wrap well with plastic wrap, and refrigerate for at least 1 hour. (It can remain in the refrigerator for a week if necessary.)

3. When the dough is chilled, dust your work surface with confectioners' sugar, and roll out half the dough at a time. Leave the remainder in the refrigerator. Roll into a circle, about ¹/₁₆ inch thick, giving the dough quarter turns as you roll, and sprinkling with a bit of confectioners' sugar to prevent sticking. Work quickly; when the dough loses its chill, it is difficult to work with.

4. Cut the circle of dough like a pie, into 16 wedges. (Cut circle in half, then into quarters, then eighths, and finally into sixteenths.) Combine the granulated sugar, raisins, cinnamon, and walnuts in a bowl. Sprinkle each wedge with the mixture and roll, from the wide edge to the point, into a crescent. Place the crescents on an ungreased cookie sheet. Refrigerate. Repeat with the second half of dough. Refrigerate for ½ hour. Preheat the oven to 350°F.

5. Bake for 15 to 20 minutes, or until lightly browned. Do not overbake; they will still be a bit soft when done. Let cool on a rack.

SOPHIE'S SAVORY TURNOVERS After rolling out the cream cheese dough, (lightly dust your work surface with flour, not sugar), cut it into 3-inch circles. Fill with browned onions (the onions should be coarsely chopped rather than sliced). Fold circles into half-moons, crimp, brush with egg glaze, and refrigerate for 15 minutes. Bake at 350°F for 15 to 20 minutes, or until golden. Serve as a first course.

UTTERLY DECADENT KUGEL

During the baking of this lokshen kugel, the brown sugar-butter mixture used to coat the baking dish caramelizes. When the kugel is turned out onto a platter, the caramelized sugar forms an almost black crust. The contrast of the dark crackly-hard crust against the white creamy-lemony interior is what makes the kugel so extravagantly good.

Serves 8 to 10

½ pound wide egg noodles
4 eggs
½ cup sugar
¾ cup sour cream
¾ cup creamed cottage cheese
Grated rind of 1 lemon
¼ pound butter, cut in pieces
¾ to 1 cup dark brown sugar

1. Preheat the oven to 350°F.

2. Cook the noodles according to package directions. Drain in a colander. Rinse well under running water.

3. Beat the eggs with the sugar. Beat in the sour cream, cottage cheese, and grated lemon rind. (If you have a lemon zester, use it to grate the lemon rind right over the bowl of ingredients, so that some of the lemon oil goes into the mixture too.) Rinse the noodles under running water once more, stirring with your hands to separate them. Add to the sour cream mixture. Toss with two spoons so that everything is well combined.

4. Put the butter in a 9 x 13-inch shallow oval glass baking dish. Place in the oven and let the butter melt. Remove from the oven and sprinkle brown sugar evenly over the butter. Mash down with the back of a fork so that the sugar melts into the butter and is evenly distributed over the bottom of the dish.

5. Pour the noodle mixture into dish. Bake for 1 hour.

6. Remove and allow to cool in the dish for 5 to 10 minutes. With a knife, loosen the kugel all around the edge of the dish. Turn the kugel out onto a serving platter. Allow to cool to room temperature. Serve at room temperature. Leftovers may be served cold from the refrigerator or brought back to room temperature.

HOT RICE PUDDING

One summer Sunday morning I ate an unforgettable rice pudding at Ratner's on New York's Lower East Side. I tried to duplicate it at home, but the rice pudding recipe in Ratner's cookbook did not produce the magical, custardy mass I had eaten that summer morning. I made rice pudding over and over again until finally I found it. If you must, add grated nutmeg, cinnamon, lemon or orange rind, but this is really at its soothing best with just the pure innocent flavors of milk, rice, vanilla extract, and sugar. The bottom layer is creamy rice, the top is custard.

Serves 6

4 eggs
½ cup sugar
1 teaspoon vanilla extract
Pinch of salt
1 cup half-and-half
2 cups milk
1½ cups cooked rice
Heavy cream

1. Preheat the oven to 350°F.

2. Beat the eggs with the sugar. Beat in the remaining ingredients except the cream.

3. Pour the mixture into a buttered 2-quart, 8-inch-square pan. Bake for 1 hour and 15 minutes, or until the pudding is set and a delicate golden color on top. Serve warm. Pass the cream.

FRUIT COMPOTE

Serve 4 to 6

¼ cup golden raisins
1 pound mixed dried fruit
1 cup dry white wine
½ cup sugar
½ cinnamon stick
Juice and rind of 1 lemon
Sour cream or whipped cream

1. Combine the raisins, fruit, 1 cup water, and the wine in a baking dish. Allow to soak for 1 hour.

2. Preheat the oven to 350°F.

3. At the end of an hour, stir in the sugar, cinnamon stick, and lemon juice and rind. Cover the dish and bake for 1 hour. Serve warm with sour cream or whipped cream.

FRUIT STREUSEL CAKE

This open-faced fresh-fruit-and-crumb-topped coffee cake is equally good as a snack or a dessert.

Makes 1

Streusel Topping
⅔ cup all-purpose flour
⅓ cup sugar
½ teaspoon cinnamon
2½ ounces butter, softened

Cake
2½ ounces butter, softened
½ cup sugar
2 eggs
¼ teaspoon vanilla extract
1 teaspoon lemon extract
¾ cup self-rising flour
⅓ cup cornstarch
4 tablespoons milk (approximately)

Fruit
4 Granny Smith apples, peeled, cored, and sliced into wedges, or 6 small ripe peaches, pitted and sliced into wedges

1. Make streusel: sift together the flour, sugar, and cinnamon. Work in the butter with your fingers until the mixture is crumbly. Set aside.

2. Butter and flour a 9 x 13-inch oval glass ceramic baking dish. Preheat the oven to 350°F.

3. Cream the butter and sugar together. Beat in the eggs and flavorings.

4. Sift together the flour and cornstarch and beat into the butter-sugar mixture with enough of the milk to make a smooth batter with a heavy dropping consistency.

5. Pour the batter into the prepared pan. Spread and smooth it with a rubber spatula. Arrange the apples or peaches over the batter in overlapping rows, leaving about ½ inch clear around the rim. Sprinkle the streusel over the whole thing.

6. Bake for 30 to 40 minutes, until the cake browns and pulls away from the sides of the pan and a toothpick inserted through the cake (not the fruit) tests done. Serve the cake, cut in squares, right out of the pan.

SOUR CREAM COFFEE CAKE

This buttery, velvety-tender cake is really best after it has cooled, but I am rarely able to keep it that long. It is adapted from that valuable little book, *Matzoh Ball Gumbo*.

1 cup softened butter
2 cups sugar
½ teaspoon vanilla extract
2 eggs, at room temperature
1 cup sour cream, at room temperature
2 cups self-rising flour
Nut mixture (recipe follows)

1. Preheat the oven to 350°F.

2. Cream the butter and sugar until light and fluffy. Beat in the vanilla extract.

3. Beat in the eggs, one at a time.

4. Stir in the sour cream alternately with the flour.

5. Put half of the nut mixture on the bottom of a well-greased and floured 3-quart bundt pan. Pour and scrape the batter into the pan over the nuts. Sprinkle the remaining nuts evenly over the batter.

6. Bake for 45 to 50 minutes. Test for doneness by pressing the cake lightly near the edge with your finger. If it springs back, the cake is done. Let cool in the pan for 10 minutes, then turn out onto a rack to cool thoroughly.

Nut Mixture

1 cup chopped pecans
1 teaspoon cinnamon
1 tablespoon dark brown sugar

Combine pecans, cinnamon, and brown sugar.

Source Guide

Russ and Daughters
179 East Houston Street
New York, NY 10002
(212) 475-4880
All manner of smoked and cured fish and other "appetizing" store specialities shipped express mail ($100 plus shipping minimum order). Inquire about Mark Russ Federman's "Fish of the Month Club."

Cumberland General Store
Route 3 P.O. Box 1056
Crossville, TN 38555
Morton's TenderQuick curing salt (write for their catalogue).
       or write to:
Morton Salt Consumer Affairs
110 North Wacker Drive
Chicago, IL 60606

Bernstein on Essex Street
135 Essex Street
New York, NY 10002
(212) 473-3900
Kosher Salamis airmailed anywhere in the United States.

Kirsch's Mushroom Company
920 Longfellow Avenue
Bronx, NY 10474
(212) 991-4977
Excellent quality dried Polish mushrooms available by mail. Inquire for current prices.

Paprikas Weiss Importers
1546 Second Avenue
New York, NY 10028
(212) 288-6117
Real Hungarian paprika; hot, medium, and mild. Write for their catalogue.

Index